The Book of Love

Through the Eyes of a Child

Calvin Wooten

authorHOUSE®

AuthorHouse™
1663 Liberty Drive, Suite 200
Bloomington, IN 47403
www.authorhouse.com
Phone: 1-800-839-8640

First published by AuthorHouse 1/7/2009

ISBN: 978-1-4343-5710-6 (sc)

Library of Congress Control Number: 2008910722

Printed in the United States of America
Bloomington, Indiana

This book is printed on acid-free paper.

Dedication

To my friend Tom, thank you for believing in me. Your friendship has been my blessing. May God bless you as you walk in His love. To the reader, may God's love and grace fill your heart full as you read this book.

Contents

Preface

By the love of God, I have been commissioned and inspired to write this book. It is a simple book written by an uneducated man. My formal education would be that of an eighth grader at best. I have no religious training and have studied at no seminaries. However, my qualifications are through life experience—thirty plus years of my life were consumed and bound by sin. I have had criminal charges that range from petty theft to attempted murder. I have been an extremely violent and angry person for the majority of my life. I would estimate the number of people I have harmed through my actions to be in the thousands.

I have dedicated the last five years of my life to loving God and all people, which is the primary topic of this book. The main purpose of this book is to give you, the reader, hope, in love and to show how this hope, when coupled with faith, can be used to open the greatest of all God's gifts. That gift is love. God installed this gift in the hearts of all people. To receive it, we simply have to use it.

As we enter into the house of God's infinite love, the mysteries of life are revealed. All truth as we know it is left at the doorstep. The physical laws of this world are suspended as we, His children, become aware of God as He manifests Himself within us. All that I have searched for and wish to be I have found, in God's infinite love.

It is in His house of love that I find rest from this world. As I rest in love, God covers me in a blanket of peace.

This peace is worth talking about, as it is a by-product of love. Moreover, it can be achieved only through love. The threat of the biggest bomb cannot produce it; likewise, there is no compromise big enough to produce peace. The definition of *peace* is not the absence of war, it is the presence of love. Peace is the very essence of love. Let this peace be our vision, and wars will end.

I believe in the hardest of hearts there is still hope In love, there is hope in peace. Have we gone so far that we cannot envision a world of peace? A world where men and women of all countries love each other? Is there a plague which condemns us to kill one another for eternity? Has there been a war somewhere on this earth every year for over two thousand years? Have we as human beings failed to bring peace? One more question: why?

I believe for there to be peace on this earth, there has to be peace in man. In addition, this requires a trinity where God, man, and love unite as one. It is in this trinity that we as people will know truth, and in this truth, our choices will be limited. We will choose God, not death. We will choose to love our fellow man, not kill him.

The effects of love are profound and extraordinary. Love has no boundaries or limits; it can touch the heart of one woman, as she gazes into the eyes of her newborn child. On the other hand, it can move the hearts of one million men to aid those in need after a national disaster. On a much greater note, love is the radio wave which tunes us into our father, our creator. It is in this achievement of love that God makes Himself known to us.

That is what this book is about—to show you, the reader, that the spiritual laws of love are as effective today as they were two thousand years ago. That in fact through love, God has made Himself known to me. Moreover, He desires to do the same to you. No matter what your past may be, God loves you and desires to be near you.

I will try to describe how this life-changing event occurred. To do this in a way that God has put on my heart to do, I will first write a biography of my life, a summing up, so to speak. I will write of things that people have done to me and of things that I have done to people, then I will write about what God has done to me. I will close this book with the final chapter being about love.

My goal and hope for this book is to set the wheels of love in motion for all those who read it. I pray that as you read this book your love for God and your fellow man will fill your heart fully, and that in so doing, the miracle of God will be made known to you.

Chapter 1:
Age 5 through 10

In the beginning of and all throughout this book, I would like to express to you the devastation in my life brought about by the progression of self-centered fear. I will express how this fear takes form, and how it can manifest into anger, rage, resentment, sexual misconduct, depression, and yes, suicide. Fear, to me, seems to be one of, if not the primary source of evil. From it stems all sorts of spiritual plagues.

The crippling effects of fear will become evident to anyone who reads this book. Through my experiences, I will show the binding affects of fear; how as a direct result of fear, I was unable to express or feel love; how living a life filled with pain seemed normal; and how fear, in fact, would keep me for years from ever experiencing God's true nature, *love*.

My purpose in this book is not to rewrite scripture or create a new type of faith, but to aid in enlarging what is already there through the application of love. I will begin chronologically with six chapters of my life to accurately describe the devastating progression of fear. I will follow with four chapters based on my walk with God in his infinite love. There will be one chapter dedicated solely to God's love.

In my earliest memories as a child, I was not taught of God. However, I believed in God. Through the eyes of this child, anything was possible with God. I had no fear of God, just blind faith.

This soon vanished and was replaced with fear.

My mother had six children, five of whom lived at home. I was too young to remember when my father left, however, I do remember when my stepfather arrived. My early memories of him were good, I liked him. The first event with him happened between age five and six: it was of him cutting my real father when he came to visit. That was probably my first experience with fear as a child. I did not understand why this happened. It seems as though fear was easily suppressed, and I continued to like and look up to my stepfather.

My stepfather had four sons who lived with us. They were all older, and the oldest was maybe sixteen. My memories of two of them are that they were mean; one of the others seemed neutral, the other, depressed. The first major event in my life that brought on fear was witnessing a fight between my stepfather and my stepbrothers. His sons where yelling at him, accusing him of killing their mother. Looking back I can now understand the depression of the one son. I was probably between the ages of six and seven when this happened. As I am writing, I am trying to recall how I felt. I can tell you that I was afraid, absolutely petrified.

As a child I had heard of people that had killed. I had even seen them on TV, but this was different. It was personal, right there, I could not avoid it. Fear, from that point on continuously reshaped my relationship with my stepfather; I no longer looked up to, respected, or even liked him. I feared him! I have seen other children in my life who, based on the love for their father, wanted to please him, and in doing so, they received their father's love. I assure you, I was not like these children. From that point on, everything I did for my stepfather was based on fear. I recall wanting and trying to please my stepfather, hoping that he would like me. I was under the assumption that if he liked me he would not hurt me.

My stepfather, at that time in my life, seems to change: he was becoming more violent. This violence was escalated by what I would now call alcoholism. He is fighting a lot with my mother and was abusive to all the kids.

The next major event in my life took place between the ages of seven and eight. The two mean stepbrothers continued to get more aggressive. This might seem common place in a family this large. What happened next is not as common. I was molested by the older stepbrother for several years and, made to do things I did not want to do. I remember wanting to speak out, to tell on him; however, being afraid of both my stepfather and my stepbrother, I did nothing.

My stepfather by this time was beating my mother on a somewhat regular basis. I wanted to tell my mother what was happing to me, but I was afraid it would cause a conflict between her and my stepfather. Looking back at this, I can almost feel the hopelessness of my situation. I became somewhat comfortable with the pain of being molested, the physical and mental abuse, and the overall violence in our home. Fear, at this time, became normal.

At this point I would like to give an overview of my behavior. My memories of my first few years of school are vague, but I do remember wanting to do well in school. Trying hard to study, I had a desire to make good grades. I remember trying to be the best in all sports: I wanted to be the fastest runner, the best kickball player, and the best football player. All these desires stemmed from one desire: I simply wanted to be loved.

I also remember getting into trouble at school. There were a few fights, and I was skipping school by now. The one thing that is most evident to me at this time is my disregard for authority: I acted out in class, I did not respect the teachers, and at times, I tried to embarrass them. I knew that I would be punished for this behavior, yet it did not matter.

A lot of people would probably say that I was seeking attention. This is half true. The other half is this: I felt as if I was being punished all the time and always by older people. I was constantly miserable. If I was to feel like this, then they should too.

Maybe this was my first attempt at fighting back. Anger, aggression, disrespect, opposition, and resentment, all this by age nine and all stemming from fear! By then I am stealing on a small scale, candy, coke bottles and such from stores.

I have written a little about punishment. I feel as though I need to describe this punishment more. There were two major types of punishment in my home. You either got whipped or put on restriction, usually both. There seemed to be only one scale to weigh the number of whippings you would receive. Everything depended on how drunk my stepfather was at that time. The severity of the crime, so to speak, did not matter. Some of these whippings literally would leave me black, blue, and with whelts from my ankles to my shoulders.

By this time in my life the oldest stepbrother had moved out of our home. I want to say I was happy, but that would be incorrect. Happiness was impossible by this time, relieved would be more appropriate. However this relief would be short lived. The second stepbrother, who I described as mean, began to molest me. This stepbrother was more aggressive and violent; he beat on me quite often.

I was probably between the ages of nine and ten at this point. By now I would be right in saying I was severely depressed. I was withdrawing from people, mostly adults. I had a hard time talking around them from fear of being punished. I believe at this age there was one of many turnings point in my life. I was introduced to marijuana. This would be the beginning of a long history of drug abuse. This drug abuse would eventually aid in my very own self destruction. However, at that time it was a well-received gift. The constant fear and pain seemed to be gone.

By now I had become interested in girls. With my new-found freedom from fear, a result of the marijuana, I was able to talk to girls, to kiss them, and even touch them in personal places. I had a drive for this behavior. I remember in my early childhood pulling a girl's shorts down as she walked by on the school bus. I think back now at how terrible that must have been for her. My sexual behavior at that time was perverted and abnormal and would continue to get worse until age thirty-six.

I was stealing a lot more as a result of my drug use. I was breaking into people's homes. Looking back at this, I cannot ever recall thinking of right and wrong or the consequences of my actions. It seemed to me that people just did whatever they wanted to do to each other.

Conclusion

- Is fear a motivating force behind sin?
  Is fear the very spirit of all that is evil?
  Can it manifest into anger, rage, resentment, sexual misconduct, depression, and suicide?
  I believe it will become evident in this book that fear can manifest.
  Note the effects of fear as it applies to my relationship with God.

- I had a firm belief in God as a child although I was not taught of God .
  In my first event with my stepfather, I overlooked fear.

- Fear has begun to reshape my relationship with my stepfather. I also believe that my God-given ability and desire to love was crushed, and this would cripple me for the next thirty years.
  Being molested adds to that fear.

- I had fear for my mother's life, (fear is accumulating).
  I am now becoming comfortable with pain and fear.
  I desperately want to be liked and loved.
  This is the beginning of an accumulation of my sins.

- In fear, I could never please my stepfather.
  I felt as if I could never measure up and would always be punished so why try. There is no happiness in my life.

- I was molested again (more accumulation of fear) I began using mood-altering drugs, developed misguided sexual instincts, and became depressed—all as a result of fear.

Chapter 2:
Age 11 through 16

I am between the ages of ten and eleven now.

My marijuana use continues and is progressing. I am stealing more because of this.

My sexual behavior has become more aggressive. I am now playing games with girls, like seven minutes in heaven, spin the bottle, and truth or dare. I seemed to like these games, however; I could not play them unless I was high. I was very shy and withdrawn otherwise.

My behavior in school is getting worse, I am becoming more verbally abusive to teachers. I remember tripping a substitute teacher as she walked past my desk. I do not recall planning this, it just seemed like the thing to do at the time. I am skipping school frequently. It was not that I did not like school, it was the way I felt while in school. For example, I remember having to do written essays as an assignment in class, and then reading it in front of the whole class. The fear of this was overwhelming: I could not do it, so I would just skip school.

The fights were getting more frequent. I remember there were a few blacks kids in our school and that the white kids would pick on them. There was one black kid in particular. His name was Andrew, and he was my best friend at the time. I always stood up for him and helped him. Looking back, I believe Andrew and I were on common ground, we both lived in fear.

I am probably eleven years old by now. The stepbrother who had been molesting me had left, and we had moved to a house in the same county. At this time, I get my first criminal charge, breaking and entering. I believe I was arrested and put in a detention center for a few weeks. I went to court and was released on probation. I would remain on some form of probation until I was forty-one years old.

By now, I am sneaking out of my house every night after my parents go to sleep so that I can get high. I had a brother that was working at a restaurant at that time and was stealing beer so that we could drink at night.

I am twelve years old now, and I had run away from home several times. One time in particular sticks out; I had left home and went to a subdivision called Lake Arrowhead. I had friends there. I believe this was my first binger. I was gone for four or five days. I stayed drunk or high the whole time. I also broke into three houses while I was there. I remember waking up one morning in a camper trailer that I had obviously broken into. What had woken me up was a girl coming in. I knew her and she knew me. Her name was Tammy. I remember her asking me, "Calvin, what are you doing here?" I looked at her confused and answered, "I do not know." This was my first black out, I then went back home.

I received my second criminal charge, breaking into a restaurant. Not just any restaurant, but my mother's place of employment. The owner of this restaurant was also the owner of the house my parents were renting. Needless to say, this was not good. I believe I was arrested and charged, but not locked up.

While waiting for my court date, I received my third criminal charge. I believe it was assault with intent to kill. I would like to give an overview of what was going on: one, the stepbrother who molested me moved back home; two, the first stepbrother who had molested me was visiting; and three, my stepfather's whippings were more frequent and unmerciful. With all that said, I'll go back to the criminal charge. I had been in the cafeteria eating lunch, and I was high from marijuana. My gym teacher, I believe, came to me and accused me of changing seats as this was not allowed. He asks me to move back, and I responded with "No, I am going to eat my lunch." A few minutes later, he came back with the principal of the school who asks me to come to his office. I responded sarcastically saying I would see him after lunch.

What happened next would again be a turning point in my life. He grabbed me by the shirt collar and pulled me up the steps. I knew he was going to take me to his office, and then whip me. By the time we got to the top of the steps I was in a rage. I had enough whippings. The voice in my head screamed, No more! I turned around and kicked him down the steps. I don't remember what I said or did after that. I only know what he and my friends said I did, and that was yelling, "I will kill you."

I remember leaving that school on that day of my own free will and knowing I would never be back again. I felt as if I had stepped into a new life that day—one of freedom. I can tell you this, I was never sexually abused again, nor would I stand passively and allow someone to beat me. If someone was going to hurt me, it was not going to be easy. I would fight back. All this at twelve years old.

When I left that school, I knew I was in trouble. I walked to my probation officer's office and turned myself in. I was locked up for close to a year. I was put in a place called Elk Hill Farm. It was a group home for trouble youth. This place did me no good whatsoever. Upon my release, my parents thought I had changed, they were wrong.

I am now between the ages of thirteen and fourteen. I now know that I was a full-blown alcoholic and drug addict back then. All I wanted to do was get drunk or high. My drug use was escalating into acid, hash, pcp, and what was called "loveboat."

My criminal history continues as I get caught for breaking into houses again. This time I stole over thirty thousand dollars worth of jewelry and a gun. I went to court, was found guilty, and again spent almost a year locked up in a place called Hanover. It was a correctional facility for juveniles.

I was put in a maximum-security cell due to the fact that I always tried to break out. I was successful most of the time, including that one. I was caught once by airplane and once by a helicopter.

I am now between the ages of fourteen and fifteen. I am released and continue to use drugs and alcohol. Stealing becomes second nature.

I am now becoming sexually active. I have a girlfriend, and she seems to like sex as much as I do. One of my friends, who lived close to us, was older—maybe twenty-three at the time. My girlfriend, me, my friend, and his wife all took acid together, then got in bed together. I had sex with my girlfriend, my friend had sex with his wife, and then we traded partners.

By now I have broken into several more houses. I had been questioned once by a detective and feel I am going to be caught. I am at school one day, looking out the window, and I see a police car pull into the parking lot. I knew they were coming for me. A few minutes pass, and a woman comes into the classroom. She asks for Calvin and said I needed to report to the office. I left that classroom and headed straight for the front door. I never looked back. I just ran.

Two days later I am a fugitive. I am fifteen, and I am on a bus headed for Oklahoma. I have an uncle there who is willing to take me in—to be my guardian, so to speak. He has all intentions of helping me. Looking back, I can see that he was a wonderful person who just wanted to help.

However, I did not think I needed help. I had a different ideal. I was going to do whatever Calvin wanted to do. I stayed with my uncle for a few weeks, then moved to a town called Chicashay, Oklahoma. I stayed with a stepbrother for a few weeks. I then found an apartment close by. I never really paid much rent at this apartment. I believe the owner felt sorry for me and allowed me to stay.

My alcoholism really took off here. I could go into bars and not be carded. Alcohol mixed with my violent nature seemed to go hand and hand. They complimented each other, and I fought a lot while drinking. I had gotten to a point that I was stealing from beer trucks on regular basis. I would wait for the driver to go into a store, and then I would steal the beer. I lived in Oklahoma for about one year. I survived solely on stealing.

I now want to write about my anger and violence. I was with a few people one night, and as a group, we decided we were going to beat and rob a man who we considered a wino. We believed he had just gotten a disability check. In the beginning, I was just along for the ride, so to speak. What happened next, would turn out to be another turning point in my life. We got into a car and headed for the railroad tracks. I had a few beers on the way, and by the time we got there, I had gone from following the pack to leading it. I got out of the car, found this man, and beat him unmercifully with a club. The others joined in. By the grace of God this man lived.

From this point on, I never followed people again. I always led the trouble.

The next major event in my life would be a riot. It was a group of white people against a group of Indians. This had nothing to do with racism. I would know because I started the whole thing. I beat a man a few nights before. We were both drunk. It just so happened he was an Indian. A couple days later, he and his friends came looking for me. This lead to a huge fight—between fifteen to thirty people.

A lot of these people would get hurt. The fight lasted for about thirty minutes and spread over two blocks.

One more turning point in my life: I will end the chapter with this one because it is a story in itself. I will pick up on it in the next chapter.

My first shot of cocaine was on my sixteenth birthday. I liked it.

Conclusion

- It is obvious I am suppressing fear with alcohol and drugs. I have no confidence with girls. I am not participating in class as a result of fear of what people will think. My anger is progressing. I seem to seek people like myself.

- I seem to have no regard for the consequences of my actions. I am an alcoholic and drug addict.

- I have become selfish and have no concern for others. I am depressed. Fear has manifested into anger, and then projected as violence.

- I was self deceived. I thought I was free of fear, but it had hid itself and had actually begun to control my life (behind the scenes, so to speak).

- I was seeking happiness through sex.

- I need help and do not know it. I seem to have no feeling of remorse for hurting people.

- I wanted people to fear me based on my own fear of being hurt.
  Fear seems to have taken its own form in this chapter, and I let it. Why?

Chapter 3:
Age 16 through 21

I am now between the ages of sixteen and seventeen, and in the previous chapter I have mentioned my first shot of cocaine and that I liked it.

I don't believe at this time it was the cocaine that I liked so much, rather the effect of the shot. The results were instant—that I liked.

I would like to write briefly about my sexual behavior at this time, as it is progressing. I met a girl, I slept with her a few times, and as a result, I caught a venereal disease from her—gonorrhea to be exact. I remember going to the clinic to be treated for this and the embarrassment I felt at the time. I was treated, and cured. I then slept with the same girl and caught it again. This is insane. I was so selfish and self-centered in my sexual behavior that it did not matter, even if I got hurt.

The next major event in my life was again a turning point. It was a fight between me and a friend. I was drunk, and he was high on Quaaludes. We got into an argument over a girl. We were on a second story balcony of an apartment complex. I was really mad at this man. He was on the second from the top step. I was on the balcony. I grabbed the rails, one in each hand, and with all my force, I kicked this man with both feet down the steps. He was airborne for more than half the way down. He then touched down and rolled the rest of the way down the steps and into the yard. To my amazement, this man gets up and comes after me. I then pick up some sort of steel weight; it was between ten and fifteen pounds. With all my force I throw it at him, striking him about mid chest. He goes down again. He later leaves in immense pain. In the beginning of this paragraph I wrote about a turning point. I would now like to write more about that.

In chapter two, I made the statement that I would no longer stand passively while people beat me—I would fight back. This attitude was fear based. I did not want to be hurt. In the events described in the previous paragraph, I never consciously thought of killing this man. What is equally as important is I never thought of not killing him. When I threw the steel weight, I was not aiming for his chest, I was aiming for his head.

All throughout this fight, there was never a conscious thought of what might happen as a result of my actions. Equally as important is the fact that the next day I had no remorse whatsoever for what I had done. Self-centered fear seems to have progressed and manifested into a hidden ability to kill without a thought. One week later, this man and I were drinking and drugging together like nothing had happened.

About one month later, I was picked up for a theft charge and questioned by a detective. I was then put in jail as they had no juvenile facilities.

I was there for about forty-five days. Forty-two of those days I was by myself as juveniles could not be with adults. I then went to court and the judge gave me two options: Leave the state, or stay locked up. I was on a bus about three days later headed for Kentucky. My parents had moved there.

I lived in Kentucky for several months with my parents. I continued to steal, use drugs, and drink. While I was there, my mother and stepfather got into a fight. It was a pretty bad one, and the house was really torn up. I would like to say that my mother was a pretty good woman—she did not drink or anything like that. She just did the best she could with what she had. It seemed to me that all of the fights were centered around my stepfather's alcoholism.

I decided to leave Kentucky. I believe had I not left I would have tried to kill my stepfather. The thought was in my head for the first time. I hated him and wanted him gone. I hitchhiked to the state of Virginia. I lived with one of my sisters for a while, and then moved in with a real brother who I went to work with.

I am now seventeen years old. I learn how to make crank. I had shot drugs before and really liked it, but could not afford it. I could make one ounce of crank for less than twenty dollars and buy everything I needed at a drugstore. This would turn out to be a near-fatal addiction one that would nearly kill me in my early twenties. Within two months, I was averaging seventy to ninety shots per day. A day would turn into two and two into three. Before I knew it, I would be up for three to four days, hallucinating from sleep deprivation and still wanting more.

Looking back at this, I can remember exactly how that felt. It was an absolutely terrible feeling, and I was convinced it was good. A child would be able to see the devastation in this behavior. Why could I not see what I was doing to myself? There seems to be a lot more to this behavior then just a drug addiction. The ingredients to this crank are benzedrix nose inhalers, hydrochloric acid, and water. Was it the chemicals I was addicted to or the feeling produced by the chemicals? At the time, I did not have the answer or the questions, I just did it.

I am now almost eighteen years old. On one occasion, I go into a restaurant, eat, and leave without paying. Three days later I was caught for this theft and searched by the police. They found crank, marijuana, and needles on me. I was charged with all four offenses and locked up. While I was incarcerated, I received more charges for breaking and entering—the ones I had fled from when I was fifteen years old. While I was incarcerated, I do not remember ever thinking of my behavior or the consequences of my behavior—whether it was good or bad, right or wrong. To me everything seemed normal. At the time I could not be tried as an adult. I was so close to being eighteen that when I go to court, they release me.

I am eighteen now. I had moved in with one of my real brothers. He is married and his wife has a sister who is living with them. This girl would become my first wife and the mother of my two children, both boys.

The next major event in my life would be my first attempt at wanting and trying to kill people. There were some disagreements between my brother, his wife, her sister (who is my girlfriend), and myself. My girlfriend and I leave and go to my sister's house to live. A day or so later, my brother, her brother, another man, and her sister come to where we are living. Their intention was to take my girlfriend with them, as she was a minor (seventeen) and in their care. However their approach seems to me to be a little off. Her brother gets out of the car wearing a pair of brass knuckles that had about an eight-inch knife somehow welded to them. The other man had a knife. My brother had nothing. It was obvious that these men had intentions of hurting me. My brother approaches first, and he provokes an argument. Midway through this, the thought hits me as loud as thunder, These guys don't know who they are messing with—kill them.

The problem I had at the time is there are three of them, two with weapons, and I had nothing. I look around; I saw a two-by-two board about six feet long on the ground. I run for it, pick it up, and start beating the man with the brass knuckles. Each time I hit him the board breaks. I then spot a pile of rocks on the ground. They are about the size of cantaloupes. I loaded up my arm with six or seven of these rocks and proceded to chase these men down with the intent to kill them.

Out of the corner of my eye, I saw the sister pulling out of the driveway and onto the road; she had my girlfriend in the car. I break from the fight with the men, and I run as fast as I can through a field to cut her off. At a full run, I jump off a small cliff and let the last rock go before my feet hit the road. It struck the driver's side door just below the window. It left a dent the size of a watermelon. I remember saying to myself, Damn, too low. The three men left.

Later that night I decide I was going to get my girlfriend. I head for their house armed with knives and a club. I am sneaking through the woods and am almost to their house when I hear my girlfriend call for me. We meet and then left. By the grace of God, she knew I was coming and left. Had she not left, I truly believe someone would have died that night.

I would like to write a little about where I was at this point in my life. My girlfriend was under the assumption that I loved her at the time and rightly so; I had told her that several times. The truth is that was impossible. A man cannot love in one moment and try to kill four people in the next moment.

In chapter two I wrote about the hidden ability to kill. What happened is that (it is no longer hidden). It seems now to be very evident. I think back on this fight, when fear, anger, and then rage all took form. I had absolutely no control of myself. I could not have stopped myself if I wanted to. I ask myself today, Why?

There were two more major events in my life at this time, involving more violence.

Keep in mind that my girlfriend is pregnant at the time. I was mad at her for something, and I decide to make her leave. I am pushing her down the road and beating her at the same time. A man pulls over to help her. He has a mentally retarded son in the car. The man and I start arguing, and then his son starts yelling. Without a moment of hesitation, I reach down and pull a survey stake out of the ground and hit his son in the head with it.

The second event involving violence would be a fight at a truck stop. A friend and I were trying to pick up a prostitute. My friend had gotten into an argument with several truck drivers. Upon seeing this, I immediately run into the woods. I am looking for a broken branch to use as a club. I spot a wooden fence, and I ripped a board from the fence. I believe it was a two-by-six and about 8 feet long. I then ran as fast as I could back to my friend. I spot the biggest man there. At a full run, I broke the board over his head. The man fell, the other men scattered, and we left. Again by the grace of God, this man lived. Again, I had given no thought to what might happen to this man. I did not care if he lived or died. Later my friend and I laugh about it.

I would like to write a little about my sexual conduct at this time as it is perverted and progressing. I am married and have a second son. By now I am forcing sex on my wife.

I am constantly buying prostitutes, and sleeping with different women from bars. By the time I am twenty-one I have met the lady who would be my second wife. I am sleeping with her one night and my wife the next. I am lying to both women.

Conclusion

- I am sexually self centered.
  I have no concern for the lives of others.

- Self-centered fear manifested into a hidden ability to kill. I have no remorse for my actions.

- I have my first thought of killing someone.
  Fear, anger, rage, and resentment are progressing.
  My drug use is progressing, without thought of why.

- I cannot see what I am doing to myself as a result of my drug use.
  I have a strong desire to feel different and do not know why. I have no morals at this time in my life.

- fear anger and rage seem to have control of me and seem to be progressing.
  I now have the mental ability and desire to kill.

- I have no ability to love.

- I am selfish and self centered to my core.
  I am starting to enjoy hurting people.

- My sexual behavior is perverted and progressing. I am constantly lying.

Chapter 4:
Age 21 through 26

At this time in my life I have left my first wife. I was living with the woman who would be my second wife. I would like to give a brief description of this lady. She was nineteen years older than me. She was to me a very nice person. She had no criminal history, and no alcohol or drug addictions.

The next major event in my life would involve this lady. She had gone out with a few of her friends simply to have fun. While this lady was gone, jealousy began to sit in. This jealousy was so subtle that I cannot remember how it started; however, it would fuel my anger until I was out of control. For several hours, my thoughts were of her sleeping with someone. At this time, I seem to have no ability or desire to reason with myself.

This woman came home and went to bed. I later woke her up and started an argument with her. Within a few minutes, I had punched her in the face and her jaw was broken. She had to have her jaws wired closed. This lady suffered for six weeks from what I had done to her. I remember having to grind her food in a blender so she could eat. I also remember making fun of her as she ate.

About two months later, this woman and I got married. At the time we seemed sure that we were in love. Looking back at this, I am amazed at how either of us could believe we were in love. How could a man abuse a woman like this and love her at the same time? How could a woman be abused like this and love the man? Were we both that selfish and fearful of being alone? Today I am blessed to know that love based on spiritual law cannot and will not do these things.

The next major event in my life would again be a turning point. I decide to go to a bar. I had three reasons for going to this bar; one, to get drunk; two, to find a lady; and three, to find a couple of men who had jumped my brother a few nights before.

While entering this bar I spot two of the men who had jumped my brother. I decide to have a few drinks. After the drinks, I start an argument with these men. I then ask them if they would like to take this to the parking lot. They agree. Once outside, I begin to run. These men chase me. All of a sudden, I grab some sort of pole and let my momentum swing me around. I then punch one of the men in his face. I remember laughing out loud after punching this guy. I again start to run; I am trying to lure these men to my truck, as I have hidden an axe handle in the back of my truck. Once these men are close enough, I grab the axe handle. I then hit one of these men as hard as I could in the center of his forehead. By the grace of God this man also lived.

The turning point in this event is this. For the first time in my life I actually enjoy hurting people. Throughout this fight I remember being somewhat happy. It was as if I were having fun.

At this time in my life, getting into fights in bars seems to be one of my primary sources of fun.

The next major event in my life would be a fight at a country club. What happened is this: a man who is at our table had gotten a little rowdy, and then he spilt a drink. I would like to say he started the fight, but that would not be true. I was looking for a fight. So, I get up from my seat and start a fight with this man. This fight would escalate into a riot that involved an estimated forty to seventy people. The bouncers of this establishment carried nightsticks, clubs, pick handles, bats, and such. This fight ended up in the parking lot. It seemed as though everybody was fighting each other. There were knives, clubs, bottles, and I know there was at least one gun. It was a rifle; one of the bouncers had it.

In this fight one of the bouncers tried to hit me with a club, but missed. I then took the club from him. I hit him ten to fifteen times on his head and back as he was lying on the ground face down. The state and county police came, and I was arrested and charged with felonious assault with intent to kill. I spent about three weeks in jail. I went to court and was released on probation, I believe. Although my intent was, in fact, to kill this man, I believe I received an easy sentence in court because it was illegal for this man to carry and use a club. As for the bouncer, I believe he spent several days, if not weeks, in the hospital. As I have been writing, I could not help think about the lives that I have touched and hurt, as a result of my actions (forty to seventy people and their families). Is all this the result of the progression and manifestations of self-centered fear?

The next major event in my life would be an overdose. I would like you to keep in mind that my wife at the time did not know I was using drugs. At that time in my life, I am selling cocaine for one of my brothers. My brother is going to Florida about every two weeks; he is picking up two kilos of cocaine and bringing them back to Virginia to sell. At the time, I really was not selling to make money, rather to support my habit. I recall having ounces of cocaine on me most of the time.

One night while my wife was in bed, I went outside behind the shed to do a shot of cocaine. It was dark so I could not see how much I was putting in the spoon. I did the shot and immediately fell to the ground; I knew I had done too much. I remember thinking if I could just make it to the house I would be okay. I pulled myself up using the side of the shed. I am using the shed to balance myself. I feel as though I have drunk a few fifths of whisky. I decide to go for the house. I immediately begin to fall. The momentum of the fall carried me about eight steps, and I land in the gravel. I then crawled the rest of the way to the house. I believe it took me about twenty minutes to get to my house. I make it to my couch and pass out.

The next three or four days I felt really foggy. I do not believe I could have spelled my name at the time. My wife never knew about this. I told her I was sick. On about the fifth day, I decided to never shoot drugs again, and I have not since. However, on that fifth day, I decided smoking crack cocaine would be okay. This addiction would last until I was thirty-six and would cause a lot of pain and suffering, not just for me, but more importantly, to others. In others, I mean almost everyone who came in contact with me.

The next major events in my life would be the death of one brother and the attempted murder of another. I would like to first give an overview of these events. The brother that is bringing cocaine from Florida gets murdered by two men. One shot him, the other beat him. I want to say all this was over a woman; however, today from my own experience, I know this is not true. The woman I am referring to at the time is a prostitute. She was dating my brother for a while, and then started dating one of the men who killed my brother.

My brother went to their house with the intention of starting a fight. This is speculation on my part; however, I believe my brother had intentions of hurting, if not killing them, as he was caring a bumper jack at the time. As a result he was shot, beaten, and died.

Now about the attempted murder of my other brother. This was done by me. Again I would like to give an overview. This brother was selling cocaine for the brother that died. He owed this brother a lot of money and refused to pay. It was my belief that this brother knew these two men was going to kill our brother. There was a lot of bad blood, so to speak, between the brothers.

After the funeral, this brother would call me and he would say, "This is your dead brother John."

Then he would ask me to meet him at the old place. He was referring to my grandfather's old homestead. It was in a heavily wooded area. There we could settle our differences simply by trying to kill each other. My response was "Tell me were you live, and I will come there," but he never would. Several month's later I found out where he lived. I then gathered a few friends who I knew would help me. They did not know my intentions were to kill my brother. We first got drunk. This to me was a primer, so to speak. I knew that once drunk my violence and rage would escalate to a point where hurting or killing people would be easy. I had a baseball bat that belonged to the brother that had passed. I remember thinking how appropriate it would be to smash my brother's head in with it.

We went to my brother's house at about 10:30 at night. I remember looking in the window and seeing my brother on his couch watching TV. There were also several other people in his house including his girlfriend, her kids, his kids, and one other man.

We went into the house through the side door. Before my brother could get up, I hit him with the bat. At this time the other man ran. I thought he was going for a gun, so I chased him. I caught him in the kitchen, and then beat him. As I was beating this man, my friends proceeded to beat my brother. When I had finished with the man in the kitchen, I went back to where my brother was. I could not see him. I remember yelling, "Where is he?" My friends would not answer. Looking back, I believe my friends knew I would have killed him, so they did not answer. Then we left. My brother had been beaten and kicked under his own couch. I believe he suffered a broken leg and rib. Looking back at these events, there are two things that really strike me: one, I had no remorse at all for hurting the one brother; and two, I had no remorse for the death of the other. I did not mourn his death until fifteen years later.

I would now like to give a general overview of my behavior. I am lying on a regular base, even when the truth would be fine. I am working full time, yet I continue to steal to support my alcohol and crack habits. I am still buying prostitutes. I am still physically and mentally abusive to my wife. I am fighting almost every weekend, and I seem to be enjoying myself. The only feelings I seem to have are anger and rage.

I am now between the ages of twenty-three, and twenty-four. I have been charged for the fourth or fifth time with driving on a suspended license. At the time I had a license in somebody else's name and had received a criminal charge in that name also. I had to appear in court on the same day for both names. When they called my name, I spoke up, and told the judge he might as well call the other man to, because I was also him. The judge did not like this; he sentenced me to in house arrest, I believe, and ordered weekly drug testing.

The next major event in my life would be going to my first inpatient treatment center. I do not remember exactly why I decided to do this; however, I believe it had something to do with the abuse to my wife. Once I was in the treatment center, I had a desire to quit using drugs and alcohol. While I was in this treatment center, I completed all the assignments that were asked of me to do. This treatment center had both men and women staying on the property. I remember constantly wanting to sleep with the women. I finished this program. I had stayed clean and sober for twenty-seven days. I do not remember feeling good for any of these days—depressed and withdrawn would be more accurate. I believe I smoked crack the day after treatment.

I am now at the age of twenty-five. The next major event in my life would involve a fight with my wife's family and getting caught sleeping with another woman. I had been drinking with my wife's sons and we were pretty drunk. We somehow got into an argument, and then a fight. No one really got hurt that night. However I was put in jail. While I was in jail, my wife left me for the first time. Within one day I had another woman in the house. Two days later, my wife came over while I was gone and caught a woman sleeping in our bed.

My wife came back home a few days after. I later was caught trying to sleep with her daughter's best friend, and my wife left again.

I am now at the age of twenty-six. I would now like to describe as best I can what it was like on the inside of me at this time in my life. I had absolutely no concern for people. I really did not like anybody. When people would try to be my friend, I would always do something to offend them or hurt them. I am miserable and do not know it. This is mostly due to the fact that I was high or drunk most of the time. I remember having thoughts of suicide. I knew I was out of control and was okay with it. At this point in my life, everything seemed normal.

Conclusion

- I have no respect for marriage. Jealousy, anger, and violence had progressed and seem to stem from fear. All these feelings come on subtle and then explode. I have no desire to try to stop my thoughts or actions. I have no real concept of love.

- My violence is premeditated, and I begin to enjoy hurting people.

- I had a strong desire to kill and took the action. I had no remorse for this. My violence has progressed to hurting large groups of people.

- I am putting my life in danger with no thought of it.

- I am lying to my wife. I cannot see the insanity of smoking crack after an overdose; it seemed to be a good decision versus shooting drugs. I am hurting in some way almost everyone who comes in contact with me.

- I am again attempting to kill my brother. I am using alcohol to aid in my violence.

- I have no feelings of remorse.
  I have no regard for the consequences of my actions.

- This is my first attempt for a different life. My perverted sexual behavior is still progressing.

- I do not have a clue that my life is out of control. How can a man do all these things and feel normal?

Chapter 5:
Age 27 through 31

I am now age twenty-seven. I was continually getting into trouble with the law and going to jail periodically. The next major event in my life would be at age twenty-eight. I was living in the state of Virginia. My mother, who lived in Kentucky, was going to have back surgery. I decide to go to Kentucky for two weeks under the pretense that I would help my mother, as she would be bed ridden for several weeks due to her back surgery. My wife was okay with this and stayed home.

When I left my house, I immediately bought some crack cocaine. I remember telling myself it would help me stay awake for the eleven-hour drive. The eleven-hour drive to Kentucky ended up taking almost three days. I remember calling my parents and lying to them, saying that my alternator had went out in my truck, so I would have more time to smoke crack. When I finally arrived at my parent's house, I had been awake for over sixty hours. I cannot imagine what I looked like or what my parents thought.

Within three days I would meet a girl. She also was married. We started dating, and within a few more weeks, she had moved her husband out of their house and I left my wife. I went back to Virginia one time to get my personal belongings only. Within a few months I was living with this girl.

I had been with my second wife for almost eight years. I had told her that I loved her at least a thousand times. What happened to love? How could I do this to her? I had made a decision to leave my wife, quit a good job, move to Kentucky, and get into a relationship with a married woman without one sound, reasonable thought of my actions or the consequences of my actions. I just did it. I cannot help but ask myself today, Why would a man do this?

Within three months I was abusing this new girlfriend, both mentally and physically. I had caused a lot of pain and suffering to her family and mine because of this abuse. The next major event in my life would involve this woman, her sister, and my two boys. Shortly after moving to Kentucky, my first wife called and asks if I could take our boys. I agreed. After several months of controversy with one of my sisters and my second ex-wife involving a custody battle, I received custody of my two boys.

My two boys are at the ages of about ten and eleven when this next major event occurred. What happened is this: my girlfriend and I had been arguing about something—I do not remember what. She was driving down our road with her sister in the front seat and my two boys in the back seat. I am driving my stepfather's truck. I see her coming, and in a rage, I smash into her car, and then leave the scene of the accident. My girlfriend's sister was the only person who was hurt physically. Her sister suffered a minor neck injury.

I remember later that night telling myself that my boys would understand what I had done, as it was not about them, it was about my girlfriend.

This would probably be the beginning of a turning point in my life. It would be the first time that I can remember feeling guilty for what I had done. However, this guilt would be short lived, as alcohol and drugs would quickly suppress it.

I am now between the ages of twenty-nine and thirty. The next major event in my life would be a fight between my sister, her son, my girlfriend, and I. My girlfriend and my sister had gotten into an argument concerning their children. This resulted in us not speaking to my sister. About one month later, my girlfriend and I were shopping at Sears in the Jefferson county mall. I was looking at tools when I heard my girlfriend screaming for me. She was in the dressing room trying on a dress. My sister had seen her go in, followed her, and then began to beat her, while my sister's son watched.

When I arrived at the dressing room, I grabbed my sister's son by the throat and began to run with him, knocking down several clothing racks. I then shoved my sister into a jewelry display case.

By now the mall security had arrived and had us surrounded, but they would not approach me. I believe they were afraid, as I was really angry and loud. The police show up next. They ask me to stand still while they question my sister. When they were done with my sister, they began to walk toward me with my sister in the middle, a police officer on each side of her. I remember my sister having a smile on her face; it was as if she was laughing at me. Without a thought or a moment of hesitation, I punched my sister in her head as hard as I could. She fell, then slid a ways on the floor. I then held out both my hands, assuming the position. I then told the police officers to arrest me. They looked at me as if I was crazy, and then arrested me.

I remember one of the officers asking me why I hit her. He said they probably would have arrested her because she started the fight. This question stumped me. I did not know the answer so I replied, "She made me mad." I believe my sister suffered a concussion, two black eyes, and her face was swollen. I remember seeing the pictures of my sister's injuries in court. It seemed as though I had no feelings about this at all, and I was just blank.

I would now like to give an overview of where I was at emotionally at this time in my life.

Any kind of happiness is out of my reach. Everything that used to work no longer does—sex, drugs, alcohol, and fighting seem to bring more pain. However, I cannot see this. My behavior no longer seems normal. I had constant thoughts of suicide. I know I have a problem, but I cannot put my finger on what the problem is.

I decide to go into another treatment center, thinking if I could stop drinking and using drugs, I would be okay. I went into the treatment center. I was put on medication for depression as soon as I arrived. I completed all the assignments that were asked of me to do and participated in all the AA meetings. After completing the twenty-eight day program, I remember feeling worse than the day I walked in. I was using drugs and alcohol within a few days after I was released from treatment.

The next major event in my life would involve my obsession for sex. At that time in my life, I lived near Louisville, Kentucky. This city had a lot of strip clubs and massage parlors. I had heard from friends that you could go into these massage parlors and buy sex. What I would do is this: I would go to strip clubs to get excited and spend two or three hundred dollars doing this, and then I would go to the massage parlors and buy sex to settle my lust. One time they asked me if I wanted two girls. I said yes, and this cost me another two hundred dollars.

Looking back at this behavior, I cannot remember once feeling good after leaving one of these massage parlors. As a matter of fact, I felt bad. This thought takes me back to another incident in my life. I would like to write briefly about it, as it is relevant. I had bought some crack cocaine. I was at home and my girlfriend was also at home. My girlfriend did not smoke crack and was absolutely against it, so I hid my use from her. My desire to smoke crack that day was so overwhelming that I told her I was going under the house into our crawlspace to clean up, as we kept all of our Christmas and Halloween decorations in there.

I knew she would not come in there.

Once I was in the crawlspace, I did a hit of crack. Immediately paranoia set in. I stayed under the house for about one hour. I had crawled into a corner and was afraid to move. I would look out the vents in the block walls, thinking that the police were outside. The fear was overwhelming and terrible. I finally grasped enough courage to get out from under my house. I remember my first thought being, Wow, that was some good crack, and I could not wait to do it again.

I cannot help but ask the question, What could possess a man so drastically that he would continue to impose that much fear on himself? That he would continue to do things that would make him feel bad under the pretense that they will make him feel good? How can a man be that blind?

My anger and violence seem to be escalating more. I have been asked to leave my girlfriend's house because of abusing her. So I get an apartment. Again, I tell myself there is something wrong with me. I decide it is my anger. I made a decision to go to church, thinking this would help. I called my mother and ask if I could go with her. She agreed. I went to church for a while. I then made a decision to be baptized. Before going to church and being baptized, I had tried to disregard God. However after being baptized, I could no longer deny there was a God. I had a spiritual experience that night that was, to me, incredible. It also scared me. The next day I called the man that had baptized me. He said these things were normal.

I continued to smoke crack, steal, and drink. My anger had not gone away. Shortly after this I had bought my boys some presents. I believe they were Christmas presents. I later pawned them for drugs. I remember feeling bad for doing this. I also knew I could not stop using drugs. I decided I had put my boys through enough, so I called their mother and asked her to take them, which she did.

The next major event in my life would be an attempted suicide.(I am now back with my girlfriend). It would be the second attempt. The first I have not mentioned. It was when I was with my second wife. It seemed like the right thing to do at the time. The second attempt went like this: I had been smoking crack for several days, and again I had been hiding it from my girlfriend. My girlfriend had to work a late shift; she did this occasionally. I made a plan to buy some crack, alcohol, call another woman, and then party all night with this woman. I did exactly that. I went home at about two in the morning. I remember lying on my couch and thinking that I have had enough of myself. I saw no way out but to die. My girlfriend had a prescription for sleeping pills, so I took a handful. I remember praying that night. I asked God to please take my life. Within fifteen minutes, I could feel the effects of the pills. I remember that I could hear my heartbeat, and I remember waking up the next day and being upset that I was alive. As a mater of fact, I cried.

I am now at the age of thirty-one. I had constantly been in trouble with the law. I have been court ordered into anger management several times. I have also been court ordered into several outpatient treatment centers. My family has very little to do with me, and rightly so, since I have hurt most of them in some way. My thoughts are constantly of killing myself or someone else.

Conclusion

- There is a progression of drug and alcohol use.
  There is a progression of lies. I am selfish and self centered.
  I have no true concern for my mother. My sexual behavior
  is perverted and progressing.

- I have no concept of love; I use the word to get what I
  want. I have no ability to reason with myself. My anger and
  rage continue to progress.

- I rationalize my actions. I have my first feelings of guilt.
  My anger is still progressing.

- I have no concern for the consequences of my actions. I
  have no idea why I do the things I do.
  Happiness is out of reach; my search for it only causes pain.
  I am suicidal. I do not know what is wrong with me.

- I attempt to change myself, yet cannot.
  I was self deceived about happiness. I felt bad, but
  continued what I was doing.

- I continually imposed fear on myself and liked it. Why? I
  used the word *possess*, why?
  This is my first attempt to seek God.

- I no longer deny God. I have a spiritual experience, yet I
  am afraid. I fail at what I am trying to do. Why?

- I have become suicidal and homicidal. Why?

Chapter 6:
Age 32 through 36

I am now at the age of thirty-three. My drug and alcohol addictions continue to progress. My anger and violence also progress; I am continually abusing my girlfriend and other people.

The next major event in my life would involve a cocaine charge. I was trying to buy some cocaine one night, and the man I was going to make my purchase from had gotten into my vehicle. The plan was to drive around the block while we were doing our business, and then I would drop him off. A police officer saw this man in my vehicle and recognized him. The officer knew this man had an outstanding warrant for his arrest. The officer pulled us over. He searched the vehicle and found cocaine. He then arrested us.

This event for me was not that unusual. I was very familiar with being arrested. What was unusual is the fact that the man with me had tried to rob me and had shot at me twice the night before. I look back at this today and can feel how normal all this behavior felt. It was as if there was no other way to live. To me, it was no big deal that this man had tried to kill me the night before.

I cannot help but ask myself the questions, How can a man be that blind, ignorant, and arrogant that he would put his life in that much danger and believe that it is normal? How can a man believe there is no other way to live when he has not honestly tried to live another way?

The next major event in my life would involve a theft charge. I was working for a company in New Albany, Indiana. I was a forman for this company. I had access to a company truck and all the tools on the truck. I would continually pawn the tools on the truck for money to buy drugs and alcohol. I was caught stealing from this company and charged. I remember having to face this man in court. I felt badly for what I had done. However, this feeling was easy to suppress—so easy I cannot remember trying to do it. These feelings seem to take care of themselves without my awareness. Question: how can a man hurt people like this and act as if nothing happened?

By this time in my life, I have been court ordered into several outpatient substance abuse treatment facilities and anger management classes. In all these classes, I have a strong desire to change. I paid attention and participated in the class. My approach to what I thought was my problem was a head-on assault, so to speak, aided with my own self will. I failed utterly every time. What is to me equally as important is the fact that even though I was trying to change, my problems progressively got worse. The question to ask is why?

The next major event in my life would be one that lasted awhile. It would be severe depression. I would like to write about this mainly because I was unaware of it at the time. I would ride around in my truck for hours, sometimes days, smoking crack and drinking. I wanted to always be alone. After a certain amount of crack and alcohol, my mind would go blank. It was as if I were dead. The only conscious thoughts I remember would be when I ran out of drugs or alcohol. Even the task of getting more drugs and alcohol seemed more than I could bear. Occasionally I would have a thought of picking up a prostitute and sometimes of suicide. Even these thoughts would be consumed by the blankness. What is absolutely profound about this behavior to me is the fact that I am oblivious to it. I am absolutely blind to the pain and suffering I am inflicting upon myself. Only now can I look back at this and see it for what it is. Only now can I ask myself the question, Is this the progression of self-centered fear? Only now can I answer yes.

It is at this point in this book that I would like you to ask yourself the following questions: one, how can self-centered fear progress; two, how can fear manifest into anger, aggression, and depression; and three, how can fear grow like that? I would like to impose a thought; it is a simple thought, not theological. It will require you to think outside of the physical and into the spiritual. A caterpillar manifests itself, and progressively grows into a butterfly, and is no longer recognized as a caterpillar. An acorn once planted, manifests, and progressively grows into an oak tree. It is no longer recognized as an acorn. Both the caterpillar and the acorn progress, manifest, grow, and are unrecognizable as their original forms—both are considered alive. Self-centered fear seems to have the same attributes: it progresses, manifest, grows, and is unrecognizable as its original form. Is it alive?

The next major event in my life would be a letter from my mother. In a direct way, she told me I was absolutely useless and good for nothing. She stated that I would never change. She expressed the desire to never talk to me again and asked that I do not try to contact her. I knew she was right although I did not admit it. I would not speak to my mother for several years. This really bothered me, yet again, it was suppressed.

I am now at the age of thirty-five. I am continually pawning things from my house. My girlfriend has to constantly check our house to see if I have pawned our personal items. She catches me doing this on a regular basis. I decide again to go into an inpatient treatment center. The one I chose is a one-year program; it is also a homeless shelter. My girlfriend, her sister, and my stepbrother take me there. I immediately go into detox for four days. I am then told by the staff of this facility that they do not have a bed for me and that I would have to go on what they called "tour." This meant that I would have to stay at another homeless shelter until a bed was available. After talking to my girlfriend about this, I decided that was not a good idea and I went home.

The next major event in my life would be a theft charge. It would be from an employer and for ten thousand dollars worth of equipment. Stealing was not that unusual for me, however, the thought behind this theft was. I wanted to be caught. I actually wanted to go to prison. I was still on probation and had time on the shelf. In my heart, I knew that I would eventually kill someone—if just myself. It was no longer a matter of if I would, it was a matter of when.

I had decided that it would be better if I were in prison or dead. So I pawned all this equipment and went on a good binge. A detective and some police officers came to my house a few days later, but I was not there. I later turned myself in. I told the detective everything. I was then charged and put in jail. I knew that I would also be charged with probation violation. I expected it to be revoked and was okay with staying in jail. However to my amazement, I was released that night until my court date.

A few days later my sister had called. I had not heard from her for a long time. While I was talking to her, I broke out in tears. I just cried. My sister had tried to convince me to go into another treatment center. At that point, I was not willing to do this; however, after this next event, I would be. My sister had helped me more than she could ever know.

The next major event in my life would be the last one of a bad nature. It would be an assault on my girlfriend. She had said something that had upset me, and out of nowhere, I started punching her in the face. The whole time I was choking her. By the grace of God I had a moment of clarity. For once, I was able to see what I was doing. Her face was turning colors. I stopped. I left that night with nothing but a bag of clothes. My probation officer took pictures of my girlfriend's injuries the next day. I called him, and he ordered that I not go back to the house. He also said he would do everything in his power to see to it that I went to prison. However, my girlfriend did not press charges.

Two weeks later I went into a treatment center again. It was the same one that I had detoxed in. I went into this treatment center not only for recovery, but because I was homeless. I could have stayed at a friend's house for a few days, I guess. But even my friends who were like me could not tolerate me for long. I would like to stop this chapter here and go on to the conclusion.

Conclusion

I would now like to sum up all six chapters.

I will begin by saying that it has been my purpose in these chapters to show the progression of self-centered fear and how it can manifest into resentment, aggression, and anger. How these can also progress and manifest into alcoholism, drug addiction, sexual perversion, depression, and suicide—the list can go on and on. Not necessarily in this order. I have grouped these six chapters by age and major event for formatting purposes only. I assure you that my whole life since age five has been one major event. If I were to write a book describing everything that has been done to me and everything I have done to people, it would be a long book. It would also be repetitive.

To read these six chapters, it would be easy to imply that I believe all my troubles stem from one, which would be self-centered fear. This would also be incorrect. What I have not written about in length is spiritual matters. If I were to take all these problems— depression, suicide, alcohol and drug addiction, sexual perversion, lying, stealing, anger, aggression, violence—wrap them all in fear, package them in a box, and then close the box, I could then label this box with one word and everyone on this planet would know what was in that box. The word on the box would be *sin*. It is a universal language. Sin can only be matched by another universal language which would be love.

In the first epistle of John in the New Testament, it states that God is love; it also says that perfect love can eject fear. I decided to put a name on my box and mail it back. The name, I am sure you can guess, was Satan and is also universally known.

He received it and rightly so, as it was of him and by him.

What I am trying to say here is I no longer live in depression, resentment, and anger. I am no longer bound by fear or any of its attributes. I have not drank or used drugs or been in a fight in over four years. I am happy and at peace with myself and all others. Moreover, the bulk of my day is spent contemplating how I can help other people in serving God.

I know there are people in this world who have done things that seem worse than what I have written in the previous six chapters. I am equally sure there are people who have done less. It might be that a person just lies on a regular basis. Whatever the case, I believe this book can help.

It has been brought to my attention that this book could cause a lot controversy, especially in the medical field. That is exactly what it should do. Where there is controversy, there will be conversation. A doctor might ask where I got my education and how can I diagnose my depression as a fear problem or my fear problem as a spiritual problem. I can assure you that my formal education is that of an eighth grader at best. However, I have disclosed thirty years of my life, as far back as age five. Most all of these years are dedicated to a sinful life. I will disclose five more years of my life in the following chapters—all of which has been dedicated to God and love. I have very little to offer by way of head knowledge. What God has so profoundly put on me is heart knowledge—knowledge of the ability of the power of love in spiritual form. I cannot, so I will not use it to discredit people, but rather to aid in a more accurate diagnoses and solution. The question in my head is this: If we took one million people who have been medically diagnosed and treated for depression or anxiety, how many have been cured? If you took the medicine away, is the problem still there? I bet the numbers would be staggering. I would also be willing to bet that at the very least, 50 percent of these people could be relieved of their problems by practicing spiritual principals. The other side of that coin is this: I have a friend who says if a person would pray every day for ninety days—on his knees—whether he wants to or not, his life would get better. He is probably right, but who is willing to do it?

Again I would like to write that I do not wish to discredit any religious organization or organization in the business of helping people. However, I am sure there is no one organization that has the patent on building a lasting and loving relationship with God and His people. I will simply show how it worked for me in hope that it might help someone do the same.

I will now like to proceed to chapter seven. This chapter is about recovery, but not recovery from alcoholism or drug addiction or even depression. However, it is about recovering God. I will show how with the help of others I recovered what is rightfully mine, the God that lives in all of us.

Chapter 7:
Victory is in the surrender.
Year one in my journey with God.

I am now at the age of thirty-six. I have no worldly possessions, except for one bag of clothes. I have decided to go into a treatment center for the homeless because I am homeless and because I need help.

I now would like to describe what I felt like at this point. My life was shattered on the inside and out. It was as if I had taken a jigsaw puzzle of my life and scattered it on the floor of a big room. The hopelessness of putting my life together was overwhelming. Where there is no hope, there you can find pain. Where there is pain, there you can find hope. It was at this moment in my life that I realized there was nothing good about me, there was nothing worth saving, and there was absolutely nothing of myself that I cared to have. I was destructive to myself and all those about me. To me, I was broken what seemed beyond repair. How could a man possibly rid himself of himself?

Up to this point in my life, I had tried to avoid the issue of God. I acted as if there was not a God, although in my heart, I knew there was. I am sure that I feared God; I believed that forgiveness was out of reach, that I had gone too far, and had hurt too many people. I had crossed the point of no return.

I had entered the treatment part of this facility. It was based on a twelve-step program of recovery. I was three days into the detoxification stage of the program. I was laying in my bunk, thinking of all the things I had done. The pain of my past was too overwhelming. I knew I was going to cry, so I rolled over and faced the wall so no one would see. The tears came, and man did they come, and with them came more pain.

It was at that moment laying in my bunk my pillow wet from my tears, that the words came out of my mouth, "Oh, God, please help me. I give up. Whatever you want of me, I will do—just show me how." I had surrendered. God came to me at that very moment, not with words, but with a feeling. In that feeling God imposed thoughts. The feeling was one that I had never felt before. It was at that moment that I felt safer than I had ever felt. The feeling was God's infinite love. The thought that God imposed through love and ever so compassionately was this: "Calvin, my son I have always loved you, always." This part of my journey is the same as that of the prodigal son: The father did not care so much as for what the son had done. The father was overwhelmed with joy because the son was home. The father loves the son and daughter, always.

The next statement I make will be a bold one; however, it has to be made. I did not have to come to God at a church pew and confess Jesus as my savior. I did not have to be baptized, and as a matter of fact, there was no religious ritual at all. However, I am equally sure all these avenues can and do work as they apply to a relationship with God. My point being, the road is not as narrow nor is the gate as small as has been implied by men. God does not make a hard way for us, people make it hard. In my case, God was not so concerned about rituals; he was too overwhelmed with joy simply because I was coming home. God loves us all that much. With all that said,

I will say this: I am a firm believer in Jesus. I study his teachings adamantly. He is the master of love. Although, this would come one and a half years later.

Where there is pain, there you can find hope. Three days into treatment I was in enough pain that I surrendered. It was at this time that I had more hope than I had ever had in my entire life.

I had hope that my life would change. I had hope that my life would get better, and I had hope that God would come to me again. It was in that hope that my faith was born. It was at that moment, although I did not know it at the time, that my life had truly changed. It would never be the same again.

I had enough faith at that time, however small it may have seemed, I believed that God would reveal himself to me again. I wanted more then anything to feel God's love again.

I believe it was at that time that I decided God had always been seeking me and now I needed to seek God. Again, I decided there were only two ways to seek God and in both ways I could find him. I could either walk or run. Time was a luxury I could not afford so I had made a decision. I would run. From that point until now, I have sought God with all my heart. Although I did not know how to seek God, I was willing to learn. Looking back to that moment when I turned to God, I ask myself the question, What was my motivation? It is now that I can answer, love! It was that feeling I had on that third day—the one I had avoided and which had eluded me all my life. Yes, God's love had done more for me in that one day than I was capable of doing in a lifetime. Although I could not possibly grasp the fullness of what God's love had done for me that day, I can say this: I have not had the desire to drink or use drugs. I have not had the desire to hurt people since that day. Moreover, I can say this: Since that day, I have had a desire to *not* hurt people. Yes, mountains were moved that day!

The power of God's love in spiritual form should not be underestimated. In one touch, He had changed the course of my life forever. In one touch, He had penetrated and destroyed a lifetime of defenses. Yes, in one touch of God's love, He had taken a hard man and made him soft. Yes, in one touch, God had brought this man to his knees, willing to pray!

All this is what God had done for me in one day. The next statement I will make is one of fact: although God had literally moved mountains for me in that one day, I am equally sure I could have moved them back. Throughout the course of my life, God had lain at my feet my destiny, so to speak. Whether it is pain or peace was still my choice. Everything depended on one question. God had obviously done a lot for me. The question was, what am I willing to do for God? Answer: I was willing to do any and everything for God. The problem was I did not know how, but I was willing to learn. Willingness, coupled with hope and a little bit of faith, put this all into action and my journey began.

I had finished the detoxification part of the treatment program. I was then moved to another building, where I would be sleeping for several months. It is here that my treatment actually began and progressed. Prior to moving to this building, I had some preconceived notions that I would have my own bedroom with a bath and that the food would be fairly decent—not much different than the other treatment centers I had been in.

What happened is this: After arriving to this building, I was given a mat and told to sleep on the floor. As for the bathroom and showers, I would have to share them with about seventy other people. The food was an issue in itself. We could eat dinner and breakfast on the premises. When I asked about lunch, I was given a list of missions and homeless shelters where I could get a free lunch. One in particular, I remember, the guys had named it baloney alley. We would have to walk down an alley and enter a church through the back door. Once there, we could get a sandwich and a bowl of soup free, every day.

Looking back to that first night, sleeping on my mat, I can say this: I slept better that night than I had slept in years. At the time, I had no idea why I slept so well. Today, I do. It was hope. Hope has a way of stilling a shaky hand. Hope can calm the mind. In hope I found rest.

The first morning I would have to leave the property and go to what is called recovery dynamics classes. The classes were structured around a twelve-step program. Keeping the anonymity of these programs in mind, I will list the twelve steps.

1. We admitted we were powerless over _____ and that lives had become unmanageable.

2. We came to believe that a power greater than ourselves could restore us to sanity.

3. We made a decision to turn our will and our lives over to the care of God as we understood him.

4. We made a searching and fearless moral inventory of ourselves.

5. We admitted to God, to ourselves, and to another human being the exact nature of our wrongs.

6. We were entirely ready to have God remove all these defects of character.

7. We humbly asked Him to remove our shortcomings.

8. We made a list of all persons we had harmed, and became willing to make amends for them all.

9. We made direct amends to such people whenever possible, except when to do so would injure them or others.

10. We continued to take personal inventory, and when we were wrong, we promptly admitted it.

11. We sought through prayer and meditation to improve our conscious contact with God, as we understood Him, praying

only for knowledge of His will for us and the power to carry that out.

12. Having had a spiritual awakening as a result of these step, we tried to carry this message to others and to practice these principles in all our affairs.

It was through these twelve steps that I was able to start building a working relationship with God. Although I had read these steps several times throughout my life, it was only now that they began to make sense. I believe that if a person is willing and has hope, God will give him brief moments of clarity. God will light the path. However dark it may be, we only need to look for the light.

I went to all the recovery dynamics classes and participated. I raised my hand, asked questions, and tried to take advice. I was also required to go to twelve-step meetings. I went to as many as I could and listened.

One of these meetings, in particular, I would like to write about. I was probably two weeks into the treatment program. I was at a large meeting. This meeting had between three hundred to three hundred and fifty people in attendance. This meeting was so large that they had to pass a microphone around the room to those people who wished to speak.

It was at this meeting that something inside of me had prompted me to speak. Although I did not know what was prompting me, I raised my hand and awaited my turn. In chapter two, I wrote about skipping school whenever I had to do an assignment in front of the class as a result of fear.

As I awaited my turn to speak, fear began to overwhelm me. I was literally trembling. I believe I was at the verge of crying. There was that much fear. I had no preconceived notions as to what was going to happen if I spoke. It wasn't as if I were going to fall of a cliff or something of that sort. There was no logic to this fear at all. It was just there. By the time the microphone had gotten to me, I was one step away from running out of the room.

Finally they called my name, and I stood up and took the microphone. My hand was shaking so badly that as I began to speak, the microphone was punching me in the mouth. I used my other hand to steady the shaking. While I was waiting my turn, I had reached inside of myself. and found my deepest secret—the one thing I did not want to talk about. I talked about being molested. The subject of being molested is really not that important. There's not much to write about it that would do any good, so I will not write a lot about it.

What happened after talking about being molested is worth writing about. To accurately describe what happened that day, I would first like to tell a story. In chapter one, I wrote about not being taught about God, but believing in him, and how that through the eyes of this child, anything was possible. I had blind faith as a child.

I would now like to add a little more to that story. As a child—before this world and what's in it had a chance to grab me—I believed I could fly. As a child, I would run down the sidewalk, and then jump into the air. I would then hover over the sidewalk, square after square I would go. As a child, I was flying. The happiest moments of my childhood were spent flying.

The issue here is not whether I could or could not fly. The issue, the shear fact, is that I believed I could fly. When I wrote about having blind faith as a child, I meant this: as a child, there were no self-imposed boundaries on God—anything and everything was possible.

What happened on that day, to me, is nothing shy of a miracle. It was on that day that God restored me to my original state, that of a child. On that day, the chains that bound me to this earth were broken. Through the eyes of this child, anything was possible. I tell you on that day my hope had grown wings. On that day, I could fly!

After leaving that meeting, there was more peace about me than I had ever known. Although I did not know why there was peace, I did know where it had come from—it was from God. A few things happened to me that day, and at the time, I did not know what they were. Today I do, so I will write about them. The first thing was the prompting to speak at this meeting. At the time, I didn't know where this prompting was coming from, but today I do. It was a prompting by God. For once in my life, I would do something that God wanted me to do. I would like to say I did this without a fight, but that is not so. The fact is that for those few minutes awaiting my turn to speak, fear had waged a war inside of me. *Cry Calvin, run Calvin, don't speak Calvin*, were the words that kept running through my mind.

In the medical field there is a lot of talk about a chemical imbalance in a person, and a lot of different medications to solve this, and rightly so. However, here is another view. Fear had affected me mentally, as my mind was racing out of my control. Fear had affected my body in such away that it was shaking out of my control. I am equally sure that had the microphone not gotten to me when it did, I would have cried. With all that said, if there is actually a way to check the chemicals in the body, then I would bet mine were imbalanced. That is my diagnoses of myself. Here is my treatment: I spoke and fear had turned into peace!

At the time, I knew absolutely nothing of spiritual matters. That, to me, is one of the most amazing parts of this process with God. I didn't have to know anything. I didn't have to analyze it or understand it for it to work. At the time, I didn't even know why I raised my hand. I did it, and then spoke, and God produced.

`The second thing that happened to me that day is this: God gave me one day of peace, a one day vacation from life. I felt no pain that day. I would like to say that for at least a year after this day, I thought that what had brought this about with God was that I had freed myself from the molestation. I stand corrected. The molestation had happened and had long since passed. What would remain was fear and all its attributes (anger, hate, rage, violence, resentment, etc.). The molestation never had power, fear does.

What I had given God that day was my fear. The next statement is one of fact. Never has God merely taken something that I was willing to give him without giving something back. I gave God fear, and He gave me peace. What a trade. It was like trading a broken bicycle for a brand new Mercedes Benz. The same applies to giving to my fellow man. It is truly in giving unselfishly that we receive.

Throughout this book I will write about two major topics, both being spiritual in nature. One destroys spirituality, one builds spirituality. One takes life, and one gives life. Only one can eliminate the other. These two topics are fear and love.

The next thing that happened that day is this: after leaving that meeting, I acknowledged what God had done for me and thanked Him. God had let me know that he loved me. It was on this day that I began the process of falling in love with God. I wanted more then anything to be close to Him that day. If it was possible and I knew how, I would have given all of myself that day to feel the closeness to God that I now feel.

However, I had to work with what I had. Faith was obvious but not dominant. Hope that day was at an all-time high. Hope would be the driving force that would lead me to a loving and lasting relationship with God first and then people. The hope that I had that day was not blind, nor aimless. It was not for money, more friends, or even a better life. Although I had a desire to stop drinking, smoking crack, and hurting people, my hope would not rest there. My hope that day had direction, a target, and a destiny for sure. My hope rested in being close to my creator and feeling the presence of my father. With that kind of hope, there came a huge amount of willingness (another gift).

I remember going to bed that night feeling pretty good. I remember waking up the next day *not* feeling too good. I knew then I would have to continually work for this relationship with God. The twelve-step program that I was in suggested that I get a sponsor who would help me work through the twelve steps of recovery—this person being someone who had already worked the steps and had been in the program awhile. I did what was suggested and proceeded to work the steps. Never once did my sponsor say to me, "Calvin, we need to get this step done." Rather I would say to him, "I am finished. Let's go to the next." My relationship with God is my responsibility. Although my sponsor could help and guide me, the work had to be done by me. It seems to me that the amount of work that I put into this was directly connected to the amount of work God put into it. In saying that, I am sure had I procrastinated, I would not be writing this book, at least not now.

I am now about thirty days into the program and I am on the fourth step, a searching and fearless moral inventory of myself. This moral inventory had three categories. It would cover resentments all the way back to childhood, whether I thought they were still there or not. It would cover all my fears, whether it be of snakes, people, organizations, or institutions. It did not matter, I had to list them all. It would also cover my sexual conduct. I would like to give an example of this process. I would list all people with whom I was angry. It did not mater if I was still angry or not. I would then list why. Then I checked the part of myself affected. There were seven parts on the list: self-esteem, pride, pocketbook, ambition, personal relations, and sex relations. I would then check where I was to blame. For example, was I dishonest, selfish, self-seeking, frightened, or inconsiderate? Then I would write exactly what I did as a result. For example, did I punch them, lie, or cheat them, etc?

After finishing this step, I again found myself in my bunk crying. I had painted a picture of my life in detail, and I did not like what I saw. Upon completing this, I realized that at age thirty-six, I was still acting and reacting to situations as I was when I was eleven years old. I also realized my perception was off—as I perceived everybody as a threat and responded accordingly. In this, I realized that I never had a best friend. This also hurt. I also realized I was selfish and self-centered to my core. If I were to go backwards with these things, most all of them would start at fear.

There were also blessings in this process. For the first time in my life, I began to realize why I did the things I did. I realized how destructive these patterns of behavior are not so much to myself, but as it applies to my relationship with God. To destroy myself is to destroy my relationship with God. Now I had more to work with. At the time, I knew very little of what God wanted me to do; however, I knew what God wanted me not to do. He did not want me to hurt myself or others.

Next would come the fifth step. I admitted to God, myself, and another human being (that person being my sponsor) the exact nature of all my wrongs. The list was long. It went from stealing coke bottles as a child to trying to kill people as an adult. On the same day we did the sixth and seventh step. That day was a good day. The next day would be one I never forget.

I had left the treatment center that morning. I was headed for another mission—to get breakfast. It was the end of October, and it was raining. I had about fourteen blocks ahead of me to walk. As I set out for the walk, my thoughts went to God. I was in a sort of daydream mode, and my thoughts were wandering, mostly to what it would be like to be closer to God. I walked almost half the trip and had barely noticed the rain. I had paused for a moment and stood in the sidewalk. I looked up, and I could feel the rain hitting my face. And these words came out of my mouth, "Thank you, God." It was in that moment that I actually felt the presence of God for the first time. I say *felt* not only because it was emotional and mental, but it was also physical. However, it seemed mostly spiritual.

I would like to describe how this felt, although I am sure I cannot do it justice. The first thing that hit me was love, and I mean to tell you, it hit me at my core. This literally shook me. Inside of this was comfort. This comfort was beyond my understanding, then there was peace, and with that peace came joy. All these things seemed to be packaged in love, put inside of me, and then exploded. All this came on me so fast and so strong that all I could do was cry, and that was okay. These were not tears of pain, they were tears of joy. For the first time in my entire life, I would cry because I was overwhelmed with joy, peace, and happiness. I was overwhelmed by the presence of God. I would not try and stop these tears. I just let them go. The affects were so profound that they left me standing in the streets of Louisville, Kentucky, looking up at the sky in the pouring rain and crying with joy. Flying as a child could not match this day. Up to that point, it was the best day of my life.

I would like to go a little further with this and say that God had done something to me that day. In doing this, He would essentially change the course of my life. He would even change the way in which I would seek Him. A seed had been planted in me. That seed would be love. I would soon water this seed and it would grow. Although I did not know it at the time, that one day was the beginning of this book. The truth is that I knew nothing of love before that day, and on that day, all I knew was love is more spiritual than physical. I would soon learn more. Add love to faith and hope, and my willingness turned to an absolute drive. I went to bed that night happy. I woke up the next day happy.

A few days later on a Saturday afternoon, which was a free day for us as there were no classes, I was walking through the city. I had three dollars to my name. I had seen a lottery booth and decided to buy a scratch-off ticket. I won ten dollars; however, when I gave the ticket to the lady at the booth, she gave me twenty dollars. I knew she was wrong, however, I walked off. I had taken about six steps, and then I stopped. I then walked back to the lady and told her she had paid me too much. I gave her the ten dollars back. The lady thanked me for my honesty. She told me she would have had to pay that back out of her salary. While I was there, I decide to buy another one-dollar ticket. I won twenty dollars. This was good.

I had a friend with me at the time. I asked him if he would like a cup of coffee, and he said yes.

We went to a coffee shop, I asked the lady for two large cups of coffee. She gave them to us; however, when it came time to pay, she only charged me for one. Again I started to walk off, but again I turned around and told the lady she had only charged me for one. The lady thanked me for my honesty and gave me the second cup for free. This honesty stuff was really working out well, but the story is not over.

After leaving the coffee shop, I walked to the park. It was there that I saw the hotdog stand. I decided to buy two chilidogs and a coke. Again, when it came time to pay, the man only charged me for one chilidog. This time I would not hesitate. I immediately told the man he only charged me for one. This man immediately charged me for the second one, took my money, and said have a nice day. I tell you, although I had worked honesty well that day, I was expecting to get that second chilidog for free. I was still selfish and self-centered to my core. I wanted to tell that man that the lady at the coffee shop had given me a free cup of coffee for being honest and that he needed to get with the program. However, I did not, and I just left.

About thirty minutes later, it dawned on me that God had been trying to teach me a lesson that day and that he had actually given me a gift in the process. The gift was not the thirty dollars or the free cup of coffee. These were part of the lesson. The gift was happiness.

From the very moment that I turned and gave the money back to the lady at the lottery booth, I was happy. As a result of practicing a spiritual principal (honesty), I was given a spiritual gift (happiness). Happiness is a spiritual by-product of honesty.

The lesson that God taught me that day was equally as simple, yet it was extraordinarily important that I learn this lesson. Happiness had no monetary value at all, and it could not be given to me by people. I could not rely on any person, place, or thing for happiness. I would inevitably feel let down, as I did at the hotdog stand. It is not a matter of if, it is a matter of when.

Houses, cars, money, or relationships—these things are not good or bad. We do not have to have them or lose them to be happy. They simply do not have the power to produce happiness. Happiness is achieved from the inside, and then projected out. To pursue happiness through a physical world is to pursue spiritual destruction, thus eliminating our true source of happiness. A person might say I was happy when I got my new car. My response would be this: are you sure this car produced happiness, or is that your perception of happiness? My point is, how thorough have we been in our search? A man does not know what is on the other side of the fence until he climbs the fence and looks. At the end of the day I thanked God for the thirty dollars, the cup of coffee, the gift, the lesson, and the clarity to put them together.

I was about three months into my treatment, and I have to go to court for the ten-thousand-dollar theft charge. I remember getting up in the morning and doing my morning prayer. I did not pray that God help me stay out of jail or anything like that. I prayed my regular prayer. I had accepted the fact that what I had done was wrong and would accept the consequences of my actions.

One thing that was notable to me that day is this: although I was on probation, I still had time on the shelf, and was looking at my third or fourth felony charge in this state, there was no fear of going to prison. There was no fear at all. The atmosphere in the court room, to me, was odd and definitely different. It seemed that no one wanted me to go to jail. The prosecutor was okay with me paying this man back and so was the judge. The actions of the man who I stole from is a story in itself. He obviously wanted to be paid back, and I could also tell this man had an honest desire that I continue to get help. He would not hinder that in any way. He very well could have opposed my sentencing, and I would have probably gone to prison.

After court I apologized to this man. I believe we were both in tears. He then proceeded to give me spiritual advice. I tell you I was amazed. I had never seen anything like this. Here I am face to face with a man I had stolen from, and he was giving me spiritual advice. I tell you this man was love in action. This man taught me a lot that day about forgiveness as it applies to love, and for that, I am grateful. I saw this man several years later at a mall. This man said to me, "Calvin, if that is the way God chooses to use me, then so be it."

The judge ordered me to pay this man back, and then gave me more time on the shelf. This presented a problem. My restitution was four hundred and thirty dollars a month, and I could not stay at the treatment center anymore, as we could not work. After talking to my girlfriend, I went home.

I was at home for about two weeks. I continued to go to meetings and all was well. I then received a call from my probation officer. He said I had a warrant for my arrest and I needed to pick it up. He was determined that I would not go home, and rightly so. He had revoked me. I called my attorney, and he said not to worry and that he would get me out of jail the next day. The next day he told me he could not get me out and that there was a good chance I would be going to prison for quite awhile. For some reason this didn't seem to bother me. I believe I had already established a working relationship with God. I continued to pursue it while I was in jail.

I had spent about four weeks in jail. I went to court and was released into a drug court program. I truly believe it was by the grace of God that I received this program as I did not qualify for it. The program was an intensive out-patient drug and alcohol treatment program. For what it is worth, it was a really good program for those who applied it. Again, I went home.

I was now five months into my journey. I was back with my girlfriend and living with her. If I were asked at the time, how my life was, I would have answered, good. Today I would say it was better, not good. My measuring stick at the time was how long I had been without a drink or a drug. That would later change. Today, I have two measuring sticks. One is how many people have I hurt today, and the other is how many have I helped.

By this time, I had started a concrete business. I would like to say it was successful, but it wasn't. It was more like a nightmare. However, I had a drive for success. In this drive for success laid a big problem. I was devoting sixty to eighty hours a week to work, one hour a day to maintaining my alcohol and drug addiction, and only five minutes to God in prayer. In the process, I was hurting a lot of people and causing them a lot of grief. I would schedule five jobs a day and only make two. People would call and ask if I could do their job today, and without checking my schedule, I would say yes. I had a big problem with trying to please people. My intentions were good, but the effects were bad. A lot of people were upset. I actually had to go to court over this and return money so a man could finish a job.

With all that said, I don't think wanting to have a successful business is bad. However, at what cost am I willing to pay for this success? Keep in mind God has already let me know on that day walking in the rain what life could be like when I am with Him. Today, I am still not a successful businessman as the world would see it. People still get upset when I cannot do what they want when they want it, and my communication skills are not where I would like them to be. However, all this is getting better. This is my average day now: I work about eight hours a day. Inside of that eight hours, I spend about three hours contemplating love and what I can do for God and people. I then dedicate another hour to God by going to a twelve-step meeting to help someone else. In doing so, I treat my own addictions. I then dedicate another three to four hours to helping others, contemplating love, and thinking about what I can do for God and other people—not necessarily in this order, but it is done.

What I am trying to say here is that my status as a businessman has no bearing on whether I am a success or not, my relationship with God does. For the bulk of my life I had only one standard in which to judge my life, that standard being physical. Now I have two, the other being spiritual. Here is something I noticed in myself: the bulk of my life I would say, was spent in the middle-class range. Even though I smoked crack and drank a lot, I still had a fairly decent car, a decent home, and good clothes. I thought I was happy having all these things until I lost them. What I found out was this: after sleeping on the floor of a treatment center and going to missions to eat, I did not feel any different. These things did not make me feel good or bad, happy or sad.

Although I did not understand spiritual matters at this time in my life, I can say this: I had climbed the fence and began to look on the other side, the spiritual side, and in fact, the results were different. They were good. It did not take much thought to understand that the things I thought would bring happiness actually brought destruction. All these things being physical. Again, I would say most things physical are neither good nor bad. They simply do not have the power to produce the desired effects of happiness. The more I searched for happiness in the physical the further I would get from God. The further I got from God, the greater the pain. The fact is that my perception and definition of things were way off. For the bulk of my life, I had been shopping at the wrong store, so to speak. I could not buy happiness at a strip club. What I could buy there is a naked woman. I cannot buy happiness at a car lot. What I can buy there is a car.

The main point that I am trying to stress is this: maybe there should be two dictionaries in life, one for the physical definition of words, and one for the spiritual definition of words. There seems to be a lot of words in my vocabulary, words like *love, happiness, joy, peace, patience* and *kindness*. These words and more are some of the most widely misused and misperceived that I know of. These are more then just words, they are of spirit. These words have power, which stems from one power source—that source being love. As we all know, God is love.

I ask that you do not take my word on these matters, I also ask that you do not take the word of your pastor or preacher. I ask this for good reason. The truth cannot be given, it has to be found. This would be the difference between "head knowledge" and "heart knowledge." Seek and you shall find. I am asking that you climb the fence and look for yourself. Search for spiritual truth. If you're diligent in your search, you will find the truth and the truth will set you free. The amazing part of this search for truth, to me, is where you find it. It is in the heart of every person—whether they want it to be or not, it is there. A piece of God is in all of us. Question to myself: am I a successful man today? Answer: yes.

I am now coming up on one year in my walk with God. It seems as if I am constantly changing. My anger is reduced to thoughts. There are no more violent acts. There is one incident that I can write about. It involved an employee. I had fired a man that worked for me. He was very angry. He demanded that I give him his paycheck. I told him he could pick it up on Friday as usual. At about eight o'clock that morning this man showed up at my house ready to fight. This situation was really awkward. The bulk of my life I had spent fighting and hurting people and doing this relatively with no problem. I had no desire to fight or hurt this man at all. The fact is I didn't know what to do. I had never been faced with a situation like this and not responded out of anger. So I called the police. At that time, I believe as a last resort and in self-defense, I would have punched that man. However, today I believe I could walk away, and this can be done through the power of love. That Friday I paid this man. We made peace with each other, shook hands, and parted ways.

Something else I have noticed is that I am no longer depressed. For the first time in my life, I can see good things and I can see good in people. It is no longer a burden to start a new day. It is a blessing to wake up and continue my journey.

One thing I have come to terms with is the fact that I am selfish and self-centered to my core. It has become obvious to me that every problem I have had has had one thing in common and that would be me. In the beginning of this chapter I ask the question, how could a man possibly rid himself of himself? That is where I am at this point in my journey. I am determined to be rid of myself, so that I might be of better service to God and people. With God's help, this determination served its purpose. However, today I know it is not about self-elimination; it is about being selfless in a world that is selfish, and I will talk more about this in the chapter about love.

I would like to discuss one more topic before I close this chapter and that would be surrender. The title of this chapter is victory is in the surrender. I had heard a lady say this, and I knew what she meant. In the beginning of this journey, I knew there were not any good qualities evident in me. I also knew that this surrender was inevitable if I were to get better. This surrender would encompass every area of my life, even my thoughts. I would have to surrender them to make way for better thoughts.

I would like to say that I surrendered with no problem; however, that is not true. There was a problem, and that problem was fear. As I have stated throughout this book, I am not a very intelligent fellow; however, I knew that with this kind of surrender, there would be a lot of change. In this thought of change, fear was introduced. I believe this to be common in people. We fear change, and we fear the unknown. The thoughts in my head went like this: oh my gosh, my sex life will be over; oh my gosh, I'll never have fun again;oh my gosh, what will become of me; oh my gosh, oh my gosh, OH MY GOSH— do you get my point?

I really hope that this next statement grabs whoever would read this book. It is one I believe to be true. Had I not burned all of my bridges, had there been one other avenue, I would have taken it before I would have surrendered.

The next statement I make I hope will grab and hold whoever reads this book. I am almost forty-one years old, and in my life, there has been only four notably good years that I can remember. They have been the last four years. The last four years of my life have been the best four years of my life. This whole chapter has been dedicated to the first year of my journey with God. It has also been the fourth best year in my life. I say fourth because every year after this one has progressively gotten better. The fourth year being the best, and I am looking forward to next year being even better.

Is all this a result of surrender? Usually we relate surrender to defeat. However, in this surrender, I won. Victory is in the surrender. The last five paragraphs were written to give people hope in surrender. I did not have to take this to a point of being homeless; I could have surrendered long ago. Had I done so, I would have more than four notably good years.

I know I said I had one more topic to write about. When I started with surrender, however, this one dawned on me as I was writing. You might have already caught it. Fear seems to have aided in beating the last wiggle out of me. Had fear led to my surrender? Is fear the path that would lead me to God's doorstep? Is fear the emotion that prompted me to knock on God's door? Knock and the door shall be opened. One last question, does God work for the good in all things?

Chapter 8:
The Battle Begins.
The second year in my journey with God

I am starting my second year in my journey with God. This year would be different. It would involve struggles. These struggles were internal. They were inside of me. At this point in my life, there seemed to be two of me—a good Calvin and a bad Calvin. These struggles were of a spiritual nature, and were for spiritual ground. The bad Calvin, so to speak, had taken all the spiritual ground inside of me. The good Calvin or the godly side of Calvin wanted the ground back.

In chapter seven I talked about fear waging war inside of me. This was similar, but a little different. I also stated in chapter seven that God let me know that he loved me, and that I had began the process of falling in love with God. I also stated that God had planted a seed inside of me, that seed being love. In these statements lie the difference. Fear would not wage this war, love would wage war on fear. The battle had begun. As I look back at this point in my life, I can say this: fear would never impose thoughts like these (run Calvin, cry Calvin, don't do this Calvin) again. Fear would never come in the front door, so to speak, again.

It is at this point in my journey that I ran into a small problem. This problem would concern organized religion. My thinking was this: I am on this journey, and I do not belong to a church, and I am thinking that maybe I should. Here is the problem: by now, this thing between myself and God has become really personal. I do not want to mess it up. So here I have several different religions all claming to be the way, the only way, therefore making all the others wrong. See my dilemma?

There was actually a point when I thought, maybe I should go to all these churches of different religions and in so doing, surely I would be okay. This kind of thinking lasted about one month. It was toward the end of this month that I felt the presence of God again. Shortly after this the answer came to me. I did not have to believe or practice any of these religions to have a relationship with God. In fact, I already had one.

Seek and you shall find, knock and the door shall be opened— having a relationship with God is this simple. God does not make a hard way for us, again I say, people do. I decided to continue doing what I was doing. I prayed every day, I went to meetings, and I began to help other people.

One thing I would like to note is that although I had decided not to go to or practice any particular religion, I would not discredit or close my mind to any of these religions either. In fact, I would use these to improve my relationship with God. This would also aid in enlarging my ability to love all people—no matter what their faith would be and including those who had no faith.

I had begun to read a lot of different books. These books were written by people of different faiths. I did not plan this, it just seemed to happen that way. Some were by Christians, others by Catholics. I studied one that is written by the Dali lama, a Buddhist monk. The basic principle of that book was love; however, I did not find this book until my third year in my journey, so I would rather write about it in the next chapter. It was these types of books, which talked about love, that I was drawn to and would study.

I was at about fifteen months into my journey when I started working with other people, trying to help them build relationships with God.

This, to me, was a monumental event in my life. I say monumental because the effects produced by the unselfish desire to help other people and backed by affirmative actions were extraordinary.

There was one thing in particular that I noticed—I had somehow started caring about people. In fact, I believe, I had actually started the process of loving people. This only made sense because I actually loved God. I would like to say that it is a natural process that I begin loving all people, as God resides in all people. However, this is not a natural process, it is a spiritual process.

I remember I was working with a man, trying to help him, when I noticed there were tears welling up in my eyes. There seemed to be an emotion—a feeling, so to speak—attached to this desire to cry. I wanted more than anything to help this man, to give him hope and strength to move forward in his relationship with God. Keep in mind, I had only known this man for one week.

This would be love. Never in my entire life do I remember experiencing anything like this. This would be the first time that I actually loved another person. Keep in mind that prior to this, I had two grown kids. I had used this word love throughout my life mainly for selfish reasons, and the lack of spiritual knowledge.

I know a lot of people who say our feelings and emotions cannot be trusted and that we should not use them to guide us in the right direction. In fact, they can send us in the wrong direction. I agree with this kind of thinking, as it applies in a physical world. However, I used the words emotions and feelings as an example of how love is commonly perceived and defined in a physical world. Feelings and emotions are physical, but love will always be spiritual.

What I experienced for this man that day was love, and it was from and of God. I can and will say this, the fruit of the spirit—love, joy, peace, patience, kindness, goodness, faithfulness, gentleness, and self-control—all these words can be and are used in the physical and spiritual sense. In my own experience, in the physical world we feel these things, in a spiritual world we are these things; I am faithful, I am gentle, I am kind, etc.

It would be shortly after this episode of love for this man that I would realize I had never loved any person in my entire life—at least not in love's true form (spiritually). This was truly different than anything I had ever known. I don't know that I can explain it, but I will try. This experience with love was empowering, and when I say this, I mean God was present in me. Although at the time I did not know how or why God was there, I just knew He was, and in this was a new found power for me. I do not know what kind of impact this had on the man I was trying to help; however, it had a huge impact on me.

From this point on, the direction of my life would change again. From this point on, I would try to love as God loves. To think about love on this scale seemed huge, overwhelming, and at times, impossible. It meant loving all people no matter what they have done or have not done. It meant not hurting or hating people. At the time, achieving this kind of love seemed, to me, a very complicated task. However, I was willing to give it a shot. Actually, I wanted this more than anything else. What I have since learned is this: to dislike or hate one person is hard and requires more energy and effort than is required to love thousands of people.

Love has since been proven to me to be one of life's easier accomplishments. Not only is love easy, it is practical and produces far greater rewards than fear and hate. To trade love for fear is to move mountains of doubt and confusion, to change pain to peace, and to change anger to compassion. What I am trying to say hear is this: love is user friendly. Fear is not!

I am sure there are a lot of people on this earth who believe in God. I am equally sure there are people on this earth who know God. Love separates the two. Love is the difference between believing in God and knowing God. Jesus was one with the father, as a direct result of two spiritual laws. He taught to love God with all your heart and all your soul and to love your neighbor as your self. With all this said, I will say this: Love is not an all or nothing deal. Love is a learning process that takes time. It is truly in giving that we receive. I will write more about this in the final chapters on love.

I am now about one year and six months into my journey. I get a phone call from my mother, and she said my stepfather had fallen and broken and cut his arm. My first thought was, this is probably not a big deal. And it wasn't. The doctors stitched and put a cast on his arm. He later went home. About one week passes, he gets the cast off, he falls again, and the wound breaks open. My stepfather goes back to the hospital, and he gets a staff infection while he is there. He is in the hospital for over thirty days on some sort of life support. He then dies.

In the beginning of this book, I wrote about how violent my stepfather was. I later wrote that I was thinking about killing him. I would now like to say this: my stepfather ended up being an okay guy. When he passed, he was in his seventies. It was in my early twenties when I believe my stepfather and I called an unspoken truce. We never talked about the past or apologized for it, we just let it be.

I remember my mother calling again. She said I needed to come home, and that this would probably be the last chance I would have to see my stepfather alive.

Shortly after this phone call, I remember thinking about family. My thoughts went to my sister and her son, the ones I had beaten.

We were still not talking. I also believe it was at this time that I began to mourn my brother's death—the one who had passed fifteen years prior. Looking back, I think of the fights that my brother and I have been in. I will never be able to say to him, "Brother, I am sorry."

I really wanted to see my stepfather. But more than anything, I wanted to make things right with him. I wanted to say I was sorry for all I had done to cause him pain and grief. I wanted to say I love you. In the middle of all this with my stepfather, the thought came on me that I should try and make things right with my sister and nephews. Although I believed my sister had started the problems between us, I would no longer allow my pride to stand in the way. I would do my best to bring peace between us. This would turn out to be a testimony to love and a story in itself.

How it started is like this: I decided to go home, and my girlfriend, her parents, and her sister went with me. Keep in mind that my girlfriend had been beaten by my sister several years prior to this, and she hated my sister. The drive home was about six hundred miles. At about halfway, the ladies started talking about my family. They were saying things like, "They better not do this," or "They better not do that," or "if they do, I will cut them or stab them," on and on they went. I remember thinking to myself how bad all this sounded. I could actually feel the hate, anger, and fear in these people as we drove.

I remember being grateful, mainly for the fact that I did not feel as they did any longer. Even though I had not actually made peace with my sister and her sons, the thought of doing this was comforting to say the least. I remember when I thought like these ladies. I also remember how I felt as a result of thinking about bad things all the time.

I would like to talk about this for a moment. In scripture (Proverbs 23:7), it is written: "As a man thinketh, so is he." I really know what that means today. Throughout my life I thought bad things, and as a result, I did bad things and I felt bad. I thought unspiritually, and I acted unspiritually. The real kicker to me is this: I could never connect my thoughts to my actions. I could never connect my thoughts to my feelings. I could never connect my thoughts to my realities. I never really knew there was something else out there. I never really *looked* for something else either.

I would be lying if I were to say I never believed there was something wrong with me. I did believe there was something wrong, but I did not believe it was a spiritual matter. A phrase of a song comes to my mind. "Amazing Grace" is the song; the line is "...was blind, but now I see."

By the time we actually arrive, it seemed to me that my girlfriend was really upset solely due to the fact that I would try and make things right between my sister and her sons. I would be lying to say that I was not tempted to let this go and to buy into my girlfriend's anger. The thought entered my mind, Maybe she is right. It is not my responsibility to apologize. After all, she started it all.

Had it not been for one motto, I would have surely fallen for this temptation. I had heard a similar version of this motto from someone else. I then adopted it as my own. This motto, this saying so to speak, would become a code of conduct for me—an answer to all my problems. The motto is as follows: Love is the answer, what is the question? In first John, there is a statement that goes as follows: God is love. So God is the answer. What is the question? Now, I have more to work with.

Upon arriving at the hospital, one of the first persons we see is, of course, my sister. There was no initial confrontation; however, I could feel the animosity in the air. This did not seem to be the right time to make my apologies. I decided to wait for a more opportune moment. By this time, I could see and hear the anger raging within my girlfriend. She was telling me just what she thought about my sister and the idea of me apologizing. However, I was still determined.

I would later see my sister, her sons, and some more of my family in the waiting room of the hospital. I tell you God had given me a perfect moment to make my amends. I stood up that day motivated by love. In tears, I made my apologies to my family. Within minutes, love had removed years of anger, hate, resentment, and fear. Within minutes, I would be hugging my family. It was as if nothing had happened. Love was the answer, so what was the question?

Shortly after this, I would make my way to my stepfather's room where he was hooked to IVs and oxygen. Once alone, I bent down and talked to my stepfather. I told him I was sorry for all the things I had done, and for all the grief I had caused him. I told him that I loved him.

My stepfather wanted to take his oxygen mask off, but could not. He was trying to speak; however, his words were muffled and I could not make them out. We were both looking at each other through teary eyes, and love spoke for us that day. We both knew what the other thought and felt. As a child, I feared my stepfather. Thirty years later as a man, I loved my father. Did I say father? Yes, I did.

By now my girlfriend is steaming. She is out to kill me, so to speak. That day we went back to our motel, and my girlfriend's anger progressed to a point of violence. She just started punching me as hard as she could in the back. This would turn out to be the true testimony to love.

Apologizing to my sister and her sons and making things right between my father and I—to do all this amidst all the turmoil my girlfriend was causing—was a wonderful thing and a direct result of love.

However, this situation was different. Keep in mind that one and a half years prior to this I had beaten this girl really badly. I had no morals when it came to hitting women. As a matter of fact, I had no morals at all. Yes, this would be a true testimony to love. I am not talking about the love between a man and a woman. The fact is I never really loved this woman in the physical or spiritual sense. I already said I have never loved anybody. This would require something far greater—a love between a man and God.

I just kind of bent down and let this woman punch me that day. I tell you I was not angry at all. As a matter of fact, I was compassionate for this lady. It was not long ago that I thought and acted on those thoughts, as this lady did.

I tell you I was on different ground that day. There was absolutely nothing this lady could do or anybody else for that matter that could change the way I was that day. I loved that day the way God would have me love. What I learned that day is this: when you love on this level—on a spiritual level, on a level that God would have us love, and on the very level that Jesus taught—there are things you cannot do. Not because they are wrong or because any particular person said they were wrong.

That day, I could not hit my girlfriend back because on that one particular day, I loved God with all my heart and all my soul and my neighbor as myself. The spiritual law of love would not allow it. Love cannot, and so will not hurt. On this day, I was invincible.

I tell you, God had taught me a wonderful lesson that day. I am sure He set the table for me to learn. All I had to do was participate. This would be the first time that I would get a really good look at what love really is and a pretty good understanding of what love is not. This was an absolutely wonderful experience; however, it is one that would not last. The next day would bring resentment and ill thoughts toward my girlfriend. I still had a lot to learn. The plus side is that I was absolutely willing to learn. I had a feeling that God again would set the table. And he did. I felt distant from God as a result of resentment. I prayed that day for this lady and that God would direct my thoughts and actions. The resentment and ill thoughts were removed, and I no longer felt distant.

A lot of the stuff I am writing up to this point is in hindsight, so to speak. I am sure God is all over it. However, at the time I could not possibly grasp the fullness of what God was doing. Rightly so, as it would have overwhelmed me. Like I said, love is user friendly in every area.

The next part of my journey, to me, is extraordinary. As I have written, I am on this journey to find God. The compass that I am using is a little different—to say the least. It does not read north, south, east, or west. It does not read I feel good, I feel bad, I feel happy, or I feel depressed. This compass has one bearing only. It does not matter in which direction I go—the needle points to love. When I follow love (in its spiritual sense), I cannot get lost.

On this path of love, what happened next is this: I ran directly into Jesus and His wonderful message. To me, the message in itself is huge yet simple. I have already stated it—love God with all your heart and all your soul and your neighbor as yourself (neighbor meaning everybody). Inside of this message were more messages like honesty, respect, hope, etc.

It became a reality to me what Jesus had done and how He had done it. Jesus knew what was going to happen, how He was going to die, and that He was going to resurrect and have eternal life. And then He actually did it. He resurrected and walked about as He said he would.

On this one particular day, this stuff about Jesus hit me. It seemed to me that after this, I was on different ground. I believe, as a result of my own experience, there were many steps in this journey. On this day I would take another step. Faith to me says, I believe there is a God, I believe there is a Jesus. The step I would take that day would be from faith Into fact. I know longer believed there was a God, I knew there was. I know longer believed there was a Jesus, I knew there was. On this day, God and Jesus became fact.

The extraordinary part of this, to me, is how I came to this truth about Jesus. I had stepped out of the imposed boundaries of tradition; I sought this on a personal level. As I write this, I am assured God wants a personal relationship with me, and He wants a personal relationship with you.

If a person were to come to me and ask, "Calvin, if you could tell me one way in which to build a personal relationship with God, what would that be?" I would have to go with Jesus on this issue. Love God with all your heart and all your soul, and everything else will be added. This is the fundamental spiritual principal that would make all of our relationships personal. All of our relationships should and could be founded and grounded in love, provided we love God first.

I, in fact, loved my way to truth. I loved myself into a relationship with God and Jesus.

With all that said, I will say this: it took the help of a whole lot of people to do this. Some people taught me what to do, and some taught me what not to do. The one constant in all of these people is this: God works in and through people, whether people want God to or not.

I am now coming up on two years in my journey. I have decided to leave my girlfriend. I made this decision based on the fact that when I searched myself, my thoughts, and feelings, I had never loved this lady. I had, in fact, used her for my own selfish interest. If you were to ask me why at the time I did this and why I was so selfish, I would have had no honest answer. I probably would have come up with a good line or gotten angry, as to avoid the conversation. The truth I would not have known.

It was only through an honest effort at a self appraisal that I was able to face and ask God to help me be rid of these things. In a twelve-step program, this would be called a moral inventory. Self-centered fear seemed to drive most of my character flaws. As a result of fear, there seemed to be an absence of God. I would have never been able to identify this absence of God had I not first felt the presence of God. I would have instead called it pain.

The other problem I had with the relationship with this lady is this: my very presence seemed to upset her. In the beginning of my journey she seemed thrilled and supportive. In the end, I believe, she would have rather me smoke crack and abuse her. To me, this was incredible and a testimony to the two spirits at hand, love and fear, God and Satan. I chose to leave rather than to continue to cause pain.

In doing this I would again lose everything. I would lose my company, my vehicles, and almost all of my tools. I would have nothing of any monetary value. I say that I lost these things, but the truth is I never had them. My credit was shot through. Everything that I had was a result of my girlfriend's credit so she ended up with everything.

I had saved enough money to pay rent on an apartment for a few months. With the help of some wonderful friends, my apartment was furnished and all was well. Throughout this ordeal I never really got upset or stressed. I never prayed for furniture or vehicles. I never prayed for anything monetary. I stayed close to God and tried to help others..

I am almost at the end of this year, so I would now like to do an overview of this year. To read this chapter seems to imply that all was well, and that is not the truth. There were good days and there were bad days. The bad days had nothing to do with outside circumstances. They had nothing to do with my girlfriend's actions, my father's death, or the loss of anything monetary. Also, these things had no direct impact on whether I had a good day. Everything depended on my fuel source, so to speak. Would I be fueled by self or by God?

I tell you there were a lot of days that I run on self. There were times when I would plan my day or my entire week without one time asking God what He thought about my ideas. And I tell you this, there were a lot of days spent in self-inflicted pain.

There seemed, to me, to be a blessing in all this pain, so I would like to write about my experience with it. One thing I noticed is that I would always pray when I was in pain. No matter how badly I beat myself up, when I prayed God would patch me up. It would not take me long to do the math. In my mind, pain equaled peace. The next statement I make, I do not recommend to any one. In my own arrogance, I related pain to spiritual growth. As a result, I prayed for a long time for pain. In my prayers, I asked God to hit me with a thunder bolt. For a while I was in pain, although it had nothing to do with God. I continued to beat myself up. God continued to patch me up. The blessing in all this is that I stayed close to God. I knew that somehow, some way He was directly related to peace and therefore no pain.

There is a story I would like to tell. In my early twenties, I was at a bar. I was cheating on my first wife with a lady who would become my second wife. I later passed out in my vehicle with this lady in my car. I was parked the wrong way on a one way street. I woke up to a police officer knocking on my window. He had asked us to step out of the vehicle. After doing this, my wife shows up. She had been looking for me. Needless to say, there was an altercation between my wife and myself. As a result, there was also one between the police officer and myself. I ended up running from the police. I was near the river, and I knew the paths along it well, so that is where I would run. However, at the time the river was flooded, and in my drunken stupor, I ended up in it. The current was swift and overpowering. I tell you, I sobered up quick only to find out I could not get out of the river. With all my strength, I tried and tried only to fail. The river was way to strong.

The next words I would use are ones I had not used since childhood: "God, please help me." At this time I was in a lot of fear and a lot of pain. When I could not help myself, I then would call for God. I even went as far as to try and strike a deal with God. If you get me out of this river, I promise I will change. By this time, I had been swept almost one mile down the river. As if by magic, the current took me off to the side and dropped me off in a park. The water was just above my knees. All I had to do was stand up and it was over. When this was all over, I never even thanked God.

Looking back at this, I was in a huge amount of emotional pain. However, when I compared this to the pain I was in all the times I tried to commit suicide, when I stole my kids' Christmas presents, or when I was in deep depression prior to this journey, I found that all these pains were about the same. To me, this was a major spiritual breakthrough. I had always tried to put a reason behind each specific episode of pain, such as my wife left me, my car broke down, I have no money, etc. These things may be part of pain; however, in my experience, I noticed this: there were two major factors in all my pains. One, I was always involved, and two, God was always absent. In the absence of God, there will be pain. There is one constant spiritual fact that supports this: in the presence of God, there is no pain.

There is still one thing, one question, which is amazing to me. After thirty years, why did I not know this? I now ask a question to the reader: have you ever had one of those days or one of those weeks when you don't want to get up, you would rather just stay in bed, you're full of anxiety or just simply mad, yet don't really know why? We go to doctors, and they say, "Take this." We go to preachers, and they tell us all about God, and still this is not enough.

Why is it that we are so blind? My definition of blind is this: I spent the majority of my life, up to this point, doing things under the perception that they would make me happy. When after thirty years of accumulation, they aided in my self-destruction. It is kind of like smoking cigarettes. It's okay at first, until thirty years later, when you're in the hospital because you can't breathe. The doctor says, "I am sorry we are going to have to take one of your lungs." Then he asks the question, "Why do you smoke?" This is just an example. I still have both of my lungs; however, I smoked for thirty years. When my breathing got bad, I quit.

My doctor asked me, "Calvin, why do you smoke?" I tell you I was dumbfounded, I had no answer.

I can say this in complete confidence: I would have never known the truthful answer to these simple questions had I not built a relationship with God. No one could tell me this. I had to find out for myself. I was watching a television show a few months ago, when I heard a lady say that no one had proven God to her. I felt for this lady. I really did. I know that God is not to be learned or proven. He is to be experienced. In this experience, lays your knowledge, all truth, and your proof. However, there are a lot of people and organizations that can aid in this experience. However, the end result is this: my relationship with God is my responsibility. One thing I am sure of is seek and you will find, keeping in mind to love God with all your heart and all your soul. Miracles can and do happen. You are reading one.

That year had definitely been a battle. I had struggled between right and wrong, good and bad, and God or me. I remember reading a book written by Joyce Myers. In this book she talked about spiritual warfare, and she also talked about are battle position, this position being on our knees in prayer. Prayer is something I managed to do a lot of this year. There were times when driving that I would just pull over and pray. Most of my prayers were about love and how to use it. In all, this was a good year. A lot of good things happened, mostly as a result of one thing in particular—my ability and overwhelming desire to love. That whole year had truly been a gift from God. The greatest gift I could ever wish to receive God had given me that year. I am almost in tears as I write this. The gift is simple. For the first time in my life, I love other people. Feeling love from God is one thing, giving it to someone else is another. It is in giving this love that I will receive another gift or should I say spiritual law. That gift is *peace*. There is a peace coming on me that would surpass my understanding, an absolute calm. Peace is a by-product of love.

I am now at a true turning point in my life. What used to be an angry, violent, drug-addicted, alcoholic man, who was full of fear is now transforming, through the aid of God and love, into a loving and peaceful man. In the beginning of this chapter, I stated that love would wage war on fear and love won. I have felt the presence of God often this year. I have also cried a lot of tears this year, all of joy.

Thank you, God.

Chapter 9:
Lessons on Love.

I am now starting the third year of my journey with God. Throughout the past two years, I have felt the presence of and the prompting of God several times. It would be in the beginning of this year that God would initiate a very small conversation with me. In scripture it is written, "Be still and know that I am." In other books that I read, they talk about listening to that still, small voice of God. That is how it happened to me. However, the voice seemed to me to be very loud, yet loving and very compassionate. One thing I noticed is that this voice came from within me.

In this small conversation, God commissioned me to do two things: one, write a book about love, and two, before I started to write this book, God told me to be sure I could love all people. I agreed, and the conversation was over.

I would like to take a moment and write about the thoughts and feelings surrounding that conversation. The first thing I would write about is the conversation, as it would be the first time that I actually heard God's voice. I was overwhelmed with joy that day to say the least. I had long anticipated and hoped for this day, a day when God would reveal Himself more to me. I believe this was a direct result of faith and hope. Looking back to the third day of my journey, the day that I found myself in tears in my bunk overwhelmed with pain is the very day that God let me know that He loved me. God did this through feelings and imposed thought. Ever since that day, I have had a lot of hope and a firm belief (faith) that God would reveal Himself to me again. And He has, only this time it was done with words.

I believe there are two key factors other than faith and hope which would account for me actually hearing these words. One-, I had refused to impose boundaries on God. If I believed God could not or would not do things, they would not have been done—not that my thoughts have the ability to change God. However, my thoughts and actions determine how and if I will perceive and understand God.

If a man is to hear God, he must have vision. When I say vision, I am not talking about eyesight. I am talking about spiritual vision. Again, I will refer to the song Amazing Grace and the line within it, "...was blind, but now I see." This kind of spiritual vision is what I refer to. In scripture it talks about coming to God as a child, which means coming to God with no boundaries or anything that would bind us, our thoughts, or actions.

To gain this spiritual vision, it is also vital that I do my very best to make things right with people I have harmed. I must also not just forgive, but strive to love those who have harmed me. I must make living at peace with all people a top priority. All these are attributes of love.

The second thing that would aid in my ability to hear God is my love for God. By this time in my journey, I have fallen in love with God. I mean this in a literal sense. The old Calvin has fallen (God's love defeated him), and the new has risen. The new Calvin loves God deeply. I know love to be the primary spiritual source of power, that can enable us to see and hear God's miracles. I cannot help but wonder how many miracles have been unheard. I wonder how many people have prayed to God for answers to all sorts of problems, yet through their own thoughts and actions and through their inability to love God and people with all their hearts were unable to hear or see God's miracles—even though they were right in front of them. I will say this, in a state of love, I see at least a thousand miracles a day. I only need to open my eyes.

The second thing that really moved me is that God had actually commissioned me to do something, even with all the people I had harmed in my life to date, which you have read about in the first six chapters. God would commission me an angry, violent, sexually perverted, alcoholic, and drug-addicted thief to write a book about love, but only after I could love all people. This would include the step-brothers that molested me, the men who killed my brother, the father who left me, and the stepfather who physically abused me. The humor in this is in the fact that I have an eighth-grade education. My reading skills are good; however, my writing skills are very poor—thank God for spellcheck!

At the time, I had no idea why God would have me do this. The blessing is that I did not have to know why. I trusted God and accepted the task. I do not know if this book will find its way into the hands of one single reader. I do not know if this book will help one person, but if it does not, it will not be because I have not written it. And to in fact be writing this book would imply that I love all people, and that would be the truth. I do love all people including those who molested me, the men who killed my brother, my father, and stepfather. However, that would not come about until my fourth year in my journey. I will write more about it then.

Throughout this task, God has constantly given me clear direction and revealed some reasons as to why He would commission me to do this. One of these reasons is to help put love back into the hands of its rightful owner, God. In first John (in the New Testament), it states, "God is love." The definition of one is the other. I hear so many times, "I love this" or "I love that." I have heard of several types of love. Some people might not agree with this next statement, but it is an absolute spiritual truth. If it is not God-centered, it is not love. There is only one type of love and that is God's.

The second reason would be to show the healing power of love. You only need to read this book to witness that. My own testimonial is proof in itself.

The third reason to me is huge. It would be my testimonial to Jesus. It is through love that I can testify. His words are the absolute truth.

I tell you I did not learn this through some sort of lesson. It was through my experience with love that I became aware of God and Jesus. When I say *aware* I mean exactly that. I became aware. God had set the course for me in the very beginning, and that course would be love.

There is a lot written and said about confessing Jesus as our lord and savior and being baptized. These are absolutely wonderful things; however, if they are not followed by love, they are useless. Jesus clearly said we are to love God with all our heart and all our soul and our neighbor as ourself. In first Corinthians chapter 13 it states, "Though I have all faith, so that I could remove mountains, but have not love, I am nothing."

Jesus knew the way to the father, and He shared that with us. He would not have commissioned us to do something we could not do. Jesus did not tell half the truth, He told the whole truth. Am I to do just half of what Jesus said, and then assume that I am going to heaven? Jesus gave us two spiritual commandments. In short they are love God and all people. If a person could fulfill these two commandments, that person would have no need to go to heaven. Through love, heaven would come to that person. It is through love that God makes Himself known to us and rightly so (God is love). Believing in God is a wonderful thing. Knowing God is the miracle of love. I have heard so many people say, "we are not perfect" or "we cannot do that." Love has nothing to do with being perfect.

The fourth purpose is to show people that loving everybody can be done, and not only can it be done, it is actually easier to love than not to love. To read this book you would think it was a biography, but it is not. It is an unfolding of love, *most importantly a road map to peace through love.* Is this peace for just one person or the family? Is it just for the church or the entire city? Maybe a nation alone deserves this peace? I think not. Surely, God intended this peace for all people. Surely God's desire is for people to love each other through Him. It is the only true path to peace. Love and peace are manifested inside of a person first, and then projected out to others. If it is not projected out, it is not in.

I remember talking to a friend about what God had commissioned me to do, and the mention of it brought me to tears. After sleeping on this for a night, I awoke the next day ready to go to work. I replayed the tape in my head: write a book about love, but be sure you can love all people first. Although at the time I did not feel angry with anyone, I knew I did not love everyone. I was way too judgmental. Therefore, I was very selective as to who I would speak to and interact with. Writing this book was a ways off.

The task at hand was to love every person. To do this I knew I would need a lot of direction from God. This to me meant more prayer and meditation, and it meant sacrificing more of me and my time and doing for others. Two things were notable at the time: one, my desire to be closer to God, and two, my overwhelming desire for spiritual truth. Both to me seemed absolute in this business of love. I prayed to God regularly for direction and guidance. He gave me experience.

I have a passion for reading spiritual books, and up to this point in my journey, I have yet to study scripture as it applies to the Bible. This would come in the fourth year. It seemed to me that God wanted to keep me out of scripture for a while and for good reason. I will write about that in a moment. First, I will tell a story.

I am near the end of a spiritual book. I know that I am going to need another. I am contemplating reading the Bible; however, I am not sure what to do. Finally, the day comes and I am finished with my book. I open the Bible and begin to read. As I am reading, I notice that I do not understand what I am reading. It is as if I have gone completely blank. I tell you my heart was surely sad that day. All the books I have read up to this time were centered on scripture. I did not understand how this could be. I stopped reading and prayed immediately. I asked God for direction that day. Should I read the Bible or another book?

It was later that evening when I was at a twelve-step meeting that a man approached me and introduced himself. He then went on to say that his wife and he had heard me speak eleven days prior. After going home, he put a book in his car with the intention of giving it to me if he ever saw me again. It was on this day, the very day that I prayed to God for direction asking whether I should read the Bible, or another book, that through this man, God would answer my prayer and I would receive a book.

People might say this would be a coincidence—not from where I stood. This to me was a real testimonial as to how much God loves us and knows our needs. So much in fact, that He knew eleven days before me that I needed a book and had made preparations through this man to give one to me. Is it insane to think God would answer my prayer in this way? If so, would it not be in vain that we pray? One thing for sure, God works through people.

This book was written by John Ortberg. There was one key phrase in this book which was instrumental in building my relationship with God. In this book, spirituality was defined as love of God and love of man, who God so loves. This statement had meaning too it.

It was also an affirmation to me that love requires action. It is not so much in reading about God and love that I grow spiritually.

It is in my practical use of love that I will grow. The man who gave me this book is now a dear friend and has also been instrumental in building my relationship with God.

When I was near to finishing this book, I was fortunate to find another. I was in a bookstore when the title caught my eye. It was *How to Expand Love: Widening the Circle of Loving Relationships* by the Dalai Lama. I bought this book based solely on its title. I had no idea that the Dalai Lama was a Buddhist monk. In fact, I had no idea at all what Buddhism was about. I believe that to be a blessing because I was able to read and practice the meditations in this book without any bias.

Imagine this: here you have a man who says he has become aware of God and Jesus, and this same man is reading a book by a Buddhist monk. I will go further and say that I know that to be exactly what God wanted me to do. There was one particular meditation in this book that would change my whole concept of love. It went something like this: first, you take your best friend, and try and imagine all the good and happiness on this person that you can. Then, do the same to a person who is a somewhat neutral person in your life. Next, you are to do this with a person you would consider an enemy. Immediately, I went to the step-brothers who had molested me. I thought for sure I could do this. I thought for sure I had forgiven them. I tell you, I could not imagine one ounce of happiness for these men, not one!

This really bothered me. Not only had I not forgiven these people, I also found out how selective I was toward people. I gravitated toward a certain type of person. I had actually been around some people for years and not so much as said hi.

The one thing I learned is this: to say, "I forgive you," does not mean "I love you." To say, "I love you," absolutely means "I forgive you." Good things are done through love.

Although I had done considerable footwork to rid myself of resentments and to forgive people, to merely say the words to myself (I forgive you) was not enough. When asked to step it up a notch and wish well on the men who had offended me, I could not do it. My approach had been wrong. Instead of trying to forgive these men; I should have been trying to love these men.

When my brother was shot and beaten to death, I was angry and resentful for years. Although the offense had come and gone all in one day, my anger and hate had not. A person would do good to learn to love and this is why: my anger and hate for these men had grown and manifested in such a way that the pain caused by my anger and hate for these men far exceeded the pain of the original offense, the death of my brother. As a matter of fact, that same anger was projected out to hundreds of other people over a period of years. Therefore hurting them, and as a result, I was hurting myself ten-fold. We reap what we sow. It would have been far better for me and countless others had I loved these men. I tell you at the end of my rope, I met myself. It was all I could do to stay alive. I wanted to die. It is through love that I am free. Through the eye of love we do not see the offense, we see our spiritually sick and fallen brother, and we have compassion, not anger.

These are the things God would have me learn through experience before studying scripture. Therefore, I would know the truth when I read it. As I read my own writing, I cannot help but think that this approach seems backwards. However, when I read scripture today, not only do I understand it, I know the truth before I read it.

At this point in my journey, I am on an all-out search for spiritual truth. For about thirty days, I drove myself nuts as a result of this search. Finally God slowed me down just enough to let me know that I was searching in the wrong spot. The truth was not on the outside, it was always on the inside. When God built us, He installed truth as a default setting—to be used as a compass, not a whip. Some people would call this the spirit of truth. A father would never blindfold a son and drop him in the darkest of jungles with no means to find his way home. The father wants us all to find our way home—He loves us that much. I will say this, when I searched inside of myself with a lamp of love, I found truth. I had found my way home.

It was at this point in my journey that I would go to a hospital. I had a pain in my side, and I wanted to find out what was causing this pain. At the hospital, they did bloodwork, referred me to a specialist, and then sent me home. A few days later, I saw the specialist. This doctor told me my enzymes were high. She went on to explain that this could be one of two things. This doctor said to me that she believed I either had hepatitis C or the AIDS virus. There was a moment of silence. I believe the doctor sensed my unease so she began to talk. She said she would have to do more bloodwork in order to tell me what I had.

I left her office that day a little bothered, to say the least. I knew I qualified for both of these diseases; however, to myself, I was sure I had AIDS. I was not so much concerned about myself. The thought in my head was, who I have given this to? I tell you it is a terrible thing to have to think about—who have I given this deadly disease to. Especially after I have awoken from a thirty-year spiritual coma and am on a path to love.

It took several weeks to get the results of my bloodwork. I think it would be normal to say I was worried and had a lot of fear, but I did not. I knew as long as I stayed close to God things would be okay, and they were. As it turned out, I had hepatitis C. When I finally got the results, I was somewhat pleased. That was very short lived. I was later told about the treatment for hepatitis C, which was a mild form of chemotherapy, and I would have to take it for six months. The side effects of these medications were bad. They included insomnia and fatigue. Although I was tired, I could not go to sleep. There were times when I was awake for sixty and seventy hours at a time.

Another side effect was the constant feeling of being sick. I felt as if I had the flu for six months.

Up to this point, I have yet to speak of a good friend of mine. Not only is he my friend, he is also my spiritual advisor. Everything about me, past and present, this man knows. All things spiritual in my life, I run by this man. To date ,I believe, all of our conversations have involved God. What a blessing he has been to me.

I remember saying to this man, "I believe this treatment for hepatitis C is going to be a huge lesson on love." My thought behind this was that I could learn to love people even though I felt bad. I remember reading a book, and in this book it said that it was easy to be nice and treat people well when you were having a good day and everything was going your way. How about when you were having a bad day? Could you do it then? I knew I was about to have a bad six months. In my heart, I was anxious to get on with this lesson. As always, God has a whole lot more to teach me than what I think.

One of the first lessons was on trust. I am about two months into my treatment and I cannot sleep. I am staying awake for two and three days at a time. People are suggesting that I take a sleep aid. I decide to try something all natural. I tried some sort of tea and melatonin, but neither worked. At the time, I refused to ask my doctor for sleeping pills.

In a twelve-step program, there's a lot of talk about the phenomenon of craving. It suggests that if you take one drink or one drug, the craving will set in, and you will take another. And I believe that. However, when I talked to my friend and spiritual adviser, he said he thought I was wrapped up in fear. I later talked to him and told him he was right. I was wrapped up in fear. However, I did not fear becoming a drug addict or alcoholic again, I feared becoming the old Calvin again. By this time in my journey, God has fed me the good life, and I really like the taste of it.

The bulk of my life I could not stand to look myself in the mirror. To do so would only bring guilt and pain. At this point in my life, I liked what I saw in the mirror. Even though I was sick and reaching the point of sleep deprivation, I could still see what God had done. I could see the light in my eyes. I could see the love and peace that He had put in my heart. Most of all, I could see the smile on my face. Nothing of this world could make a man smile like this. This was a God-given smile.

I was willing to suffer any amount of pain. I would not lose my smile. Behind that smile was the man that God would have me be. That, to me, was worth suffering for.

My friend said he thought it would be okay for me to take prescribed sleeping pills. So I called my doctor, and he prescribed me Ambien. My girlfriend had to drive me to pick up the prescription. I remember the doctor saying that I would be asleep in a few hours. Several hours later, I was still awake. I called the doctor back, and he prescribed another medication. This one was Xanax and these are highly addictive. I took them, and at about eleven that night, I was sitting on my couch, and I knew I was high from these pills. I could feel it. It was at this point that God came to me, again in a voice. He said to me, "Calvin, nothing can ever make you feel as good as I can." I knew this to be true. That night I was intoxicated from the pills; however, I did not like it. I had no desire at all to feel differently. I will say this: to this day, I still look in the mirror and like what God has done. I still have my smile. Sometimes I walk away, then turn and go back to the mirror to see it one more time. Every now and then I will do a little happy dance, and then thank God for all He has done.

My first lesson on love was to trust God. That is where love begins and never ends! The second lesson really caught me by surprise. It revealed to me how much pride and ego I still had and how much I still feared people. The second lesson was on how to let people love me. In my thinking, I believed that it was not spiritually correct to ask or accept help from other people. However, throughout these six months, people constantly helped me. They constantly asked how I was doing and if there was anything they could do to help. People prayed for me. For the first time in my life, I would let people get close to me. Finally it dawned on me that people actually love me. Then there were tears. I liked the way it felt to have people love me.

The third lesson to me was monumental. There was no price big enough to put on its value. I would like to take a moment and try and describe what it was like at this point in my treatment. When I started this medication, I was almost at two hundred pounds. Toward the end, I was at 153 pounds. I weighed more than this as a full-blown crack addict. To me, it looked as if my bones were going to pop out of my skin. Although I was taking sleeping medication, I still could not sleep. There were times when I was awake for fifty to sixty hours at a time. To the outside world, I looked very sick.

This is the result of the third lesson. On the inside of me, there was a peace beyond me. I tell you there was happiness and joy on the inside. I was unshakable, my foundation was on solid rock. Although, at the time I should have been exhausted and ready to collapse, I had all the energy I needed. I continued to go to twelve-step meetings and constantly worked with other people. Moreover, I was actually nice to people.

It was almost at the end of this treatment that I finally began to notice God's presence. All the nights of lying in bed, not able to sleep, my thoughts were constantly of other people and what I could do to help them. When I was well and feeling good, I was not capable of this constant thought of others. God had taken my mind, gathered all my thoughts, and then He directed them for me.

In the middle of the worst sickness I had ever known (other than spiritual sickness), I would feel better than I knew was possible. Is it in giving that we receive? It would have never dawned on me to be so selfless and to think more of other people. Especially in this kind of sickness, when the normal thought is to take care of yourself. God had affirmed what I believe to be true (love is the answer, what's the question?). Again I have to say, thank you, God.

Although I had begun to notice what God was doing for me, I could not grasp the fullness of His blessings until I was off the medication for a while. I began to see day by day what God had done for me. Equally as important, I began to feel what He had done. Gradually, I became aware of his presence for the entire six months. If was as if God had nursed me, as a mother would nurse a newborn child. The only difference was that God would do His nursing, so to speak, on the inside. Everything that I needed He supplied. The peace, joy, and happiness were from Him, the creator of all good things. Not only did He give me the energy to move about, he preserved my smile that I might take it with me. My constant thought of others were not my thoughts, they were His thoughts. The unshakable foundation was God!

In the beginning of this chapter, I wrote that I had felt the presence of and the prompting of God several times. However, nothing could compare to the kind of awareness that I knew after this treatment. I did not believe God was present; as a direct result of love, I knew He was present.

It was as if God had written me a letter and posted it on my heart to let me know He had been there. It went something like this.

Calvin,

While you were gone, I thought it would be nice if I took care of your house for you, so when you returned home, you would find it in order. So when I noticed you were tired, I gave you strength. When I noticed your thoughts were making you sicker, I directed them toward others so that you might know peace and the constant source of happiness that comes from loving others. The light in your eyes, I decided to leave on at all times; you can use it as a lamp to find your way home on the darkest of nights. My child, when I looked in your mirror and saw your smile, it brought tears to my eyes. I know it came from seeking me. Calvin, I hope that I have not been too invasive. However, you did ask your will be done, not mine, and I knew, in your heart you meant what you said.

P.S. The fourth and greatest of all lessons:
I am your father and I love you

Love always, God

In closing this chapter, I would like to say a few more things. In the beginning of my journey with God, I had hope that I could be closer to Him and know him better. I had no idea that it could be like this. I have since learned that there is always a higher level of awareness of God, and love is the elevator. The next chapter will be dedicated to becoming aware of God.

Chapter 10:
Becoming Aware

The bulk of this chapter will be dedicated to the varying experiences and levels of becoming aware of God throughout my journey. I believe it to be of extraordinary importance that a person identifies this awareness of God, then call it what it is. In several books that I have read, there is talk of feeling the presence of God, becoming one with God, having a conscious contact with God, and becoming aware of God. The list goes on and on.

With all that is said about becoming aware of God, when we speak of this matter, people scatter. Friends and family—who have walked the spiritual path with you, who have read and heard the same books, and talk of this awareness of God—the very people who would vow that they trust you with their lives might now look at you as if you have lost your mind. Some will distance themselves from you. Friends and loved ones might talk of you and try to discredit you. People will say God does not work like that. Your pastor might tell you, "God only burns bushes for Moses. These kinds of miracles God will not perform any longer." They might say that you have gone astray and have been misguided. The same people might proclaim to you what God will not and does not do. The very people who would help build your faith might now unconsciously try to destroy it. I write each and everyone of these things because they have happened to me.

If you are going through something similar, I beg of you to stand firm. I believe this to be Satan's last major stand. Throughout this journey, there has been a constant struggle within me—a boxing match, so to speak. A fight between right and wrong, good and bad, God and Satan. In the beginning, I thought this fight was with me. I have since learned that it is for me. That's right, we are the prize. Satan wants us, and our father loves us. Throughout my life, I have heard we can only serve one master. You will love the one, and hate the other. My job has always been to choose. I make these choices when I go into a strip club or massage parlor. I make this decision when I intentionally hurt my brothers and sisters, when I lie, cheat, or steal, the list goes on and on.

I also make this decision when I claim what God has done to me and for me. I believe when a man becomes aware of God's presence, claim's it, and then proclaims it to others, this would be the knock out punch, which would allow God's perfect love to eject fear. God moves in, Satan moves out. Every now and then, Satan comes back. Only now, I can see him. Because of my awareness of God, I have also become aware of Satan.

I would now like to go back to the beginning of this journey for a moment and recapture how I became aware of God and the varying stages of the growth of this awareness. On the third day, the very beginning of this journey, I called on God in tears and in immense pain. God answered with compassion. He let me know with certainty that He loved me no matter what. I have to ask, was this a miracle? The impact of this changed and restructured my whole life. It was not just a miracle, it was a burning bush. Thank God, I still believe in miracles. I acknowledged what God had done that day, and I have yet to stop thanking Him.

A few weeks later I was prompted to speak at a meeting. I spoke about being molested. I wrote about this in the seventh chapter. That day, I was given a day of peace. That day, I knew this peace was a gift from God. How did I know that? How did God let me know? Why did God let me know this peace was from Him? I acknowledged what God had done for me that day and thanked Him. God's impact on me was so profound that day that I began the process of falling in love with God. Was this a miracle? It was more than a miracle (it was a burning bush).

A few weeks later, on my way to a mission for a free breakfast, I found myself standing in the streets of Louisville, Kentucky, looking up to the sky, in the rain, thanking God for all that He had done. Looking back over my life, there were times when God was present, and I did not know it. However, on this particular day, God would make sure I knew He was there. Within seconds, I was overwhelmed with joy, peace, comfort, happiness, and most of all, love. I tell you, I was flooded with spiritual emotions. All I could do was cry. I was not crying because of the happiness or peace; I was crying that day because that is all I could do. I felt the overwhelming presence of God that day and my entire body wept.

I called on God that day to simply thank Him. He responded by coming to me. With Him were an army of angels. We call them the fruit of the spirit. After this day, my life again changed. A seed of love had been planted. Was this a burning bush? No, the whole forest was on fire. Up to this point in my life, I had no idea that things like this could happen. I had not been taught the pros or cons about issues with God. I believe this to be to my benefit, as I was able to come at this thing with God with an open mind. I came into this journey with the mind of a child, knowing nothing, but willing to believe.

I was a few months into this journey when I felt this presence of God. At the time, this day seemed huge. I am now four years and eight months into this journey, and that day seems small in comparison to the awareness that I now have with God. My only comparison is it is like looking into the sun. I can only take it for seconds, and my entire body weeps in the omni-presence of God. This happens to me on a regular basis. The feeling is pure, uncut love. All that I am and will be for God depends on this life-giving supply of love.

A person might think that there is some long, drawn-out theological solution as to why these things are happening between God and me. I assure you there is not. My relationship with God has been relatively simple. Faith, hope, and love are the primary principals. In first Corinthians, chapter 13, it states: "And now abide faith, hope, love, these three; but the greatest of these is love." This scripture says to me that faith and hope are stepping stones to something far greater, love. In the beginning of my walk with God, I had a lot of hope and faith. In order for these to be successful spiritual tools, I had to believe in them, I had to believe in faith, I had to believe in hope, and I had to believe in miracles.

I was so far gone at the beginning of this journey that death seemed like a real good option. I cried God's name and asked for help. Not only did He help, He let me know who was helping. I went to a big church last week primarily for direction on how I could be of service to God and people. I talked to one of the elders of this church. He asked me how I came to know God. I told him my story, and this man said to me, "God does not do that anymore." I could not help but wonder how many people he has taught that same message, the message of what God does not do. I wonder how many people, who have been blown up with so much hope that they could float to heaven, have been popped, grounded, and then nailed down by this message of what God does not do.

The next chapter of this book is the primary purpose as to why God asked me to write this book. It is a chapter on love. This chapter has been written in hope of clearing a path for the next chapter to be effective and allowing the healing powers of love to work.

The path that needs to be cleared is in our thinking. I tell you, I am the type of man who if I think about something to long, I can really complicate the simplest of matters. Something that would require little effort on my part now becomes strenuous and tiresome. Faith and hope, to me, seem to be simple concepts—almost childish. They require little effort, yet yield great dividends. Their greatest asset is belief. When I say belief, I mean belief in God and all of His miracles, including the burning bush.

For sure, Satan will go to any lengths to keep us in the dark, to blind us, and to take us to our death. You can bet our heavenly father will go to any length to give us life. He is not willing that one should perish, rather, that all should have eternal life. No miracle is too big or too small for the father's love.

Belief is the magic that allows us to hear God's voice; it is one of the essential ingredients that helps us feel and become aware of God's presence. Without belief, we will be bound to this physical world. It is through belief, faith, hope, and God that we can achieve the greatest of all spiritual gifts, love. Through the eye of love, we become aware of God's inner dwelling presence within us. Knowledge, wisdom, and truth are poured out upon us; we are no longer bound to the physical world. We can now see things physical and spiritual.

There are a few things I would note before closing this chapter: one, I have constantly acknowledged God and thanked Him for all that He has done throughout this journey. In doing so, I am losing sight of myself. Two, Everytime I acknowledged God, things change that allow me to grow spiritually. Three, sometimes the answer to a question is so easy that we miss it altogether. We struggle to find it, even though it is there in front of us. All the times that I have called on God He has made the way easy for me. I have come to trust and rely on God. What I have learned is that I do not need to figure this out because God has done that for me. When I start trying to figure spiritual matters out, I then lose sight of them. They are still right there in front of me, I just cannot see them. One example would be my work truck; at any given time, I might be pulling ten thousand pounds. I trust and rely on my truck. Without a thought, I start it and go. Now, if I had to stop and try to figure out how my truck was going to do this, this would really complicate a simple matter.

This is how it worked for me. I came to God with a childish faith and a childish hope. As a result, I came to love and began to mature spiritually. There were things that I firmly believed, and through love, I found out that they were not true. Just because I believed, that did not make it so. Just because thousands of people believe in something, that does not make it so. Love will always tell you the truth. I think deep down in each and every person exist that one big question: Is there a God? And if so, they want proof. I cannot do that for a person; however, I can help you prove God to yourself.

I know there are a lot of people on this earth who believe in God, and belief is the beginning of all good things. However, if you want to know God without a doubt, you must learn to love. The next chapter is dedicated to love. I hope that it brings you as much happiness as it does me.

Chapter 11:
About Love

I feel so blessed to be able to write this chapter on love, to look back over my life as I have done in the first six chapters, to see clearly the path of absolute destruction that was caused by me, and to see in hundreds and thousands the people I have harmed and affected through sin. And to know that without love, I would still be blind to these matters. I feel so honored to serve God in such a way. I feel honored, and it makes me happy to say I chose God.

I also feel so blessed to look back over the last four years and eight months of my life and see so clearly and definitively what God has done. Moreover, I am blessed to know that it all started with, "Son, I have always loved you," which was prompted by the prayer, "oh God, please help." I am blessed to see and feel the impact that this love has had on me and to know in my heart the endless capabilities of such a love. This love is one that is founded in God.

As I write this chapter, I will have to cover a few other topics, as these topics affect our ability to love and these very things are hidden from us. The first topic would be on spiritual blindness.

Spiritual blindness, to me, is the inability to see things for what they really are. Throughout out my life I have constantly deceived myself. When I smashed into my girlfriend's car (with my children in the car), I convinced myself that they understood it was not about them. It was about my girlfriend, therefore, it did not matter if my girlfriend got hurt, as long as my boys understood it was not about them. The next day, it was as if nothing happened.

Not long after this, I stole my kids' Christmas presents. I then pawned them for crack cocaine. I remember acting as if nothing happened when they came home. By the next day, this was no big deal. Almost all of the women that I have been with I have hurt and beaten, and I could rationalize in my head that they deserved it. Throughout all of these events, I knew I was an alcoholic and drug addict. At most times I thought this was the major problem. At other times, I thought my anger was. At any given time, I could not actually put my finger on the problem. Never would I have guessed my anger to be a manifestation of fear; never would I have called this a spiritual problem; never, and I mean absolutely never, would I have guessed Satan to be behind the scenes.

So, here I have four topics to talk about. A- deception's B- the inability to identify the problem C- the normality of things D- my complete unawareness.

I will talk about deception first. How could I rationalize my actions like this? What is there inside of me that could possibly believe I was justified in doing some of the things I have done? Why is it that I am absolutely blind to the consequences of my actions? Whether there is jail or prison time involved or even death—mine or someone else's— these things seem to not matter at all. I am constantly assured by myself that I am going to be okay, and all this after trying to commit suicide four times. How can I deceive myself so easily?

Now let me talk about my inability to identify the problem. On several occasions, I have been in treatment centers, anger management, and I have seen a psychiatrist. At all of these places I was told that I was the problem. I tell you I just could not get it. Again, I was absolutely blind. I was convinced these people were worse off than me. Even though I was in immense pain, there was something inside of me that always said, you were the problem, not me.

I cannot help but ask the question, how can a man be this blind to an obvious problem? Life is definitely not going well for me, and I can convince myself it is a fluke. How is it possible for a man to convince himself he is right, when every time he has been wrong? Why is it now I see these things clearly, but five years ago I could not?

It seems to me every time I got close to the problem, I would without recollection divert my attention or myself somewhere else— maybe a bar, maybe a strip club. Sometimes I would just get angry with someone. That way my attention would be on them, not me. If you have not noticed, all these things are unspiritual in nature. As a result, I always felt worst, never better. Again, I was blind to this. Most of the time I did not even know I was feeling bad. A good question to ask is why it did not dawn on me to do something spiritual, to simply try to do something good for a person, to be nice, and help someone?

What now seems to me to be an absolute giveaway is the fact that the lifestyle that I was living seemed normal to me. Even though at times, I would have rather been dead, I could not see another way to live. Although, at times I had hope that there was something better. After several treatment centers and a head-on assault at trying to fix myself, I settled for thinking this is normal. How can this be? How and by what means can a man concede to himself that the life he leads is normal and therefore okay?

The bulk of my life has been spent desiring things of this physical world. As a result, I could only see and perceive physical things. I was completely unaware of all matters spiritual. In fact, I was blinded by my own selfishness. I could not see spiritual things or unspiritual things. I was truly unaware of these matters, therefore, to me they were none existent. In the Gospel of Luke 11:24 it states, "When an unclean spirit goes out of a man, he goes through dry places, seeking rest; and finding none, he says, I will return to the house from which I came." That scripture implies that there are two major types of spirit: one unclean and another clean, one good and one bad, one of God and one of Satan. It also implies that I am but a house for spirit. Imagine the humbleness that has fallen upon me, as this spiritual truth becomes a reality to me. Man in all of his knowledge to create and destroy is but a house for spirits far greater than himself. Whether they be clean or unclean spirits, they are both beyond me. Moreover, to know the course of my life is determined by my choice, which master shall I serve? Will my house serve Satan or God?

For thirty years, my house had served Satan; as a direct result, I have been on a mission to kill myself and harm as many people as I could. My perception was so far off that I blamed the world and its people for all of my problems. Several times in this book I have stated that God works through people. It is now that I can say Satan also works in and through people.

For thirty plus years, Satan has hid himself from me; he is truly a master of deception and disguise. Although I could never see him, he was right there all the time; he had disguised himself as me! All the pain and suffering I had inflicted on myself and others, and I have to say that at times, I seemed to enjoy it. Is all this a direct result of which master I chose? Had I in fact become one with Satan?

I know from my own experience that to talk about Satan on this level makes people uncomfortable. Some people might say that I have lost my mind; others might deny the existence of an evil spirit altogether and rightly so. Who would want to say, As for me and my house, I will serve Satan. Very few, I am sure. The other part of that is this: evil spirits work in absolute darkness. They do not disclose themselves. There have been periods in my life when the pain was so overwhelming that my desire was to change at any cost, and still I failed.

Deep, deep down inside of me I knew I was broken, and I really wanted to be fixed. I would always be directed away from the problem. I would tell myself, "Calvin, it is your anger, work on this." Then my lust would escalate and my attention would be directed there, then my alcoholism and drug addiction, next my lying and stealing. This was one big, viscous circle, always leading back to the same spot—which was nowhere! I will go further and say that I have read several books. One said that selfishness is the only sin and from it stems all others. Another said fear is the big problem, and yet still another implied that pride and ego were the big factors. I have to concede that to identify these problems is of paramount importance, but to dwell on them would lead back to the same spot—which is nowhere. Watch out for the diversion.

This to me has proven itself to be a matter of spirit, whether they are clean or unclean. I would now like to go back to the beginning of the verse I referenced in the gospel of Luke (when an unclean spirit goes out of a man). Why and by what means would an unclean spirit leave a man? I would now like to refer to another passage in scripture, the first Epistle of John, chapter 4 verse 16: "And we have known and believe the love that God has for us. God is love, and he who abides in love abides in God, and God in him." Verse 18: "There is no fear in love; but perfect love cast out fear, because fear involves torment. But he who fears has not been made perfect in love." Is this to say that love cast out unclean spirits? And he who abides in love abides in God and God in Him. God moves in, Satan moves out.

I would again like to tell a small story. I live on a small farm away from the lights of the city. At night when I turn out the lights to go to bed, it is completely dark. The only thing that I can actually see is the darkness. At any given time, when I turn on the light, the darkness disappears. However the things that were in the darkness do not; I see my bed, my dresser, and my nightstand. When God's love turns on the light, the darkness disappears, and we see things as they are, spiritual and unspiritual.

Again, I will refer to the third day of my journey. God came to me through His love because I had none. In doing so, He turned on a light that would allow me for a brief moment to see things as they are (spiritual) for the first time in my life.

To become one with God, we must first become aware of God. How could we do this if we did not first house a spirit? All of this awareness and oneness is done only through love that is motivated by hope and catapulted by faith. Deny yourself the opportunity to not believe in the power of love. Before you refuse, first try and love God and all people, and see for yourself what is produced.

Now I will go to the next topic: Attributes of an unclean spirit.

I am writing about this topic in hopes of helping a person identify a common problem that is hugely misdiagnosed. In so doing, I hope to eliminate the viscous circle that first leads away from the problem and then right back to it. I have hope that this topic will challenge people to think about what they are made of, what it is inside of them, and what makes them who they are. Take five minutes and try to think of yourself as two pieces: one part body (house), one part spirit (clean or unclean). Now try and separate the two in your mind. How does this make you feel? If you are anything like me, uncomfortable would be a good answer. I believe this uncomfortable feeling to be an attribute of an unclean spirit, the very one that would have you pack your bags and run, only to find yourself several years later (maybe this time on your death bed) asking the same questions and feeling the same feelings. I assure you, I write every word of this because I have been there and have come through it on the clean side of things.

I have to say, as I have been writing this book, I anticipated writing a lot about God and love, but I had no idea I would be writing so much about Satan or evil spirits. Although in the first six chapters, I could feel the pull of something negative. I still had no idea where this would go. I have used the word Satan to put a name on what this accumulation of evil is. By no means has God revealed his name to me, only his character. I have used the name Satan because it is synonymous with all things evil and is known worldwide. In scripture (Matthew 4:10) it states, "Then Jesus said to him, away with you Satan! For it is written, you shall worship the lord your God, and Him only you shall serve."

There are two reasons why I referred to this scripture. One, because Jesus identified Satan, which to me is very important. In my journey with God, I believed things would be revealed to me. I assumed they would all be spiritual in nature, meaning good things. As always there is more to God than I could possibly know. As a result of becoming aware of God (and how this feels to my body), I have also become aware of Satan (and how that feels to my body). The bulk of my life was spent serving Satan, and I have always known what that felt like; however, I had nothing to compare that to. Therefore, it became a normal feeling and unidentifiable. As my awareness of God has increased, I have become aware of this flow of unclean spirit (Satan) into my body (my house). Before I could ask Satan to leave, I had to first know he was there. Not only has God's love pulled me from the gates of hell, He has given me the spiritual tools to assure that I never go back.

The second reason I referred to this scripture is in the last part of it. It is written, "you shall worship the lord your God, and Him only you shall serve." Not only was it written, now Jesus has stated it, and Him only you shall serve! This statement by Jesus raises the bar for every man and woman. This statement to me is not a command, rather an achievement. It is within the grasp of all men and woman. It is verifiable through the words of Jesus and proven through the power of love.

The reason I write about this scripture is this: I have heard so many people say we are not perfect, and that all men have sinned and fallen short of the glory of God. I bet I have heard this at least one hundred times, if not more. The same people who say this might be caught in a repetitive cycle of unspiritual behavior. This kind of thinking can bind a man. If our job on this earth is to choose and then serve, do the results of our service not belong to the master? Perfection is none of my business. If our father wills it, then it will be done. Again, I would say watch out for the diversion. Satan will have a man think highly of himself after hurting hundreds of people, and the next thought can be of suicide.

In my journey with God I have heard so many people say what God does not do. God does not pay light bills or house payments. I have heard people give their testimonies as to how God has come to them. Whether it be through voice or visions, one person I know said God came to him through the voice of a spirit, and yet another said it was through a bird—that's right, I said bird. I have also seen the hope and faith of these people destroyed by the message, "God does not do that anymore." Since Christ, God has gone from performing miracles on a regular basis to not being able to pay a light bill. It was just today that I saw a televangelist on television. He went on and on about what Satan could do, in and through people. However, he made short work of what God could do. Watch out for the diversion.

Last week I injured my leg, and I was given a prescription for pain. I was also given some papers describing the side effects of this medication. As I thumbed through these papers, I ran across one that listed the symptoms of a stroke. It listed five or six of these symptoms including the following; numbness in the arms or legs, numbness on one side of the body, a change in vision in one or both eyes, and a few others. I cannot help but wonder how many people have misdiagnosed themselves in saying, "My leg is numb, I must have poor circulation," or "My vision is blurred, I will set up an appointment with an eye doctor." I wonder how many people have died from a stroke, and their last thought was "I need glasses?" The symptoms of a stoke have been listed in order to save lives. Why? Because lives have been lost to the stroke, not the symptoms.

I made this analogy because the same thing happened to me. I misdiagnosed myself spiritually. I stopped at the symptoms. I always told myself anger was my problem, or alcohol and drug addiction were my problems, the list can go on and on. Because of this misdiagnoses, I found myself trying to commit suicide four times, and then accepting that as okay. For me, the life-threatening problem was always a matter of a unclean spirit.

These symptoms—are they the attributes of an unclean spirit? Can I use these attributes as a road map to the source of the problem?

Again, I would like to tell a little story. As I have stated in the early chapters, my stepfather was aggressively violent. When he asked a question, it would be good to have the right answer. As a child, I would get into a lot of trouble. My stepfather would always ask, "Why did you do that?" Most of the time my answer would be, "Because." In anger he would say, "What do you mean *because*? In tears knowing what was going to happen to me, again I would reply, "Because." This would result in a beating that would—most of the time—leave me black and blue with welts that would raise my skin. As a grown man, I wish I knew then what I know now. I surely would have told the truth rather than suffer those beatings. The fact is, I was as honest as I could be at the time. The best answer was, "Because," since I did not know why I did the things I did. This is how Satan works. He will take the life of a child and mangle it, leaving the child with no ambition or desire to live. Do you know I child like that? Then Satan will take the mind of the father and tell him that he is justified in doing what he has done. Do you know a father like this? I do, he is writing this book. One more small story and I will get to my point.

As I have stated, I have two children, both being boys. They are now twenty and twenty-one years old. For a long time they would have nothing to do with me, and rightly so, I stole their Christmas presents. They would not see me for seven or eight years. My oldest son would be first. I made my amends to him and all seemed well. However, my youngest would have nothing to do with me. He was angry with me and thought I was worthless. After several attempts on my part to try to build a relationship with my son, he would not have it, so I left it alone. About three months ago, I get a phone call. It is my son, and he says to me, "Dad, I want to get to know you." I remember after that call sitting in my chair in tears thanking God for what He had just done. Three weeks later, my son came to visit me for the weekend.

I decided this would be a good time to make my apologies. When we were alone, I began to apologize for the things I had done—for smashing into him in the car, for stealing his presents, and so on. Then he stops me mid-sentence and says, "Dad, I was not mad at you for those things. I was mad at you for beating up my brother." I tell you, my heart dropped as I remembered what I had done and how I had justified it. In the beginning of this chapter, I talked about spiritual blindness. Thank God I can now see. For the first time in my life, I could tell my son I loved him, and I knew for sure, it was the truth. I told my son that day that I did not know how to be a father, but was willing to learn if he was willing to teach.

I have heard so many times that men like me do not change, and to people in general, that probably seems true. However, through my own experience, I wanted to change. I wanted to be fixed; I just did not know what was broken. I no longer wanted to hurt people, I didn't want to be a alcoholic and drug addict anymore; however, in looking back, I do not see how I could be anything else. After several failed attempts at fixing what I thought was the problem, I agreed with the general public: men like me do not change. In chapter six,

I stated that I thought I would be better off dead or in prison. What a thought.

On the third day of this journey, I asked God (clean spirit) to please help. I said I give up. Whatever you want of me I will do, just show me how. My life has not been the same since that day. Unknowingly, I addressed this on a spiritual level. I chose and became willing to serve God. I will say this, the man who would beat up his son no longer lives in this house. That spirit has been evicted; I am a new man, not changed but new.

For sure, there are two major players in this world of spirit, God and Satan. For sure, God creates and Satan destroys. With that said, God created our bodies, and in doing so, He gave us the ability to feel. Most of my life I would have considered this a cancerous plague; however, it turned out to be a blessing. The attributes of an unclean spirit are all things bad—anger, violence, murder, lust, greed, lying, stealing, cheating, self-centered fear, alcohol and drug addiction—the list can go on and on. There are so many in fact that we can become confused. In this smoke cloud of confusion, Satan hides.

Here is how our father loves us: keeping in mind, God is the creator. He created then installed a spiritual law within us (we will reap what we sow). Again, I would have considered this spiritual law a cancer of some sort because it seemed to cause that much trouble. In sowing the seeds of Satan, I reaped pain (a feeling). As it turned out, pain is God's calling card. It was in pain that I called on my father. The vast majority of people I know have called on God while in pain.

God created spiritual law to aid us in finding our way back to him, not to punish or destroy us. He loves us way too much. Our father works for the good in all things. He is the creator called love.

Now would be a good time to pause and ask yourself the questions: do I suffer from anyone of or several of these attributes of an unclean spirit? Do I lie? Do I lust? Am I angry? Do I cheat? The list goes on. Have you tried to fix these problems? Have you failed? On the other hand, have you ignored them altogether? Now the big one, how do these questions make you feel? Again, if you were anything like me, uncomfortable would be a good answer. One more question. Why do I feel uncomfortable? Now would be a good time to think outside of the circle. Is the answer a matter of unclean spirit? To know the truth (not believe it), to absolutely know it, we must learn to love God and all people.

Now I will proceed to the final topic prior to love, which is the effects of sin.

To talk about sin, I believe it would be helpful to separate it into two classes, the effects physical, and the effects spiritual. I would first like to talk about the effects of sin in the physical sense.

Sin in the physical world could be considered crimes or laws. These crimes are met by punishments. The severity of the punishment depends on the severity of the crime. The severity of the crime usually depends on the amount of pain or harm inflicted on another person. For example, the punishment for murder would be harsh; it could be met by the death penalty or a lengthy prison term. Whereas an assault charge might be punishable with a few days in jail or a fine.

The same principal would be applied to a theft charge. If you rob a bank, you will go to prison. If you shoplift at a grocery store, you will probably be fined and put on probation.

What about lying? If you lied in court, that would be perjury and could be punishable by jail time. On the other hand, could you imagine trying to bring charges on a person for lying to you? We would probably be laughed out of the courthouse. Now, what about the seven deadly sins (pride, anger, lust, envy, greed, gluttony, and sloth)? Pride, lust, envy and greed—all these have earning capabilities. Therefore, they cannot be that bad. I have never heard of anybody going to jail for gluttony or sloth either.

Let us talk about lust for a moment. Is it not the sin that would lead the priest to molest the children of his perish? What about the mother or father that would molest their child? Is this motivated by lust? I remember one time when I was molested. I had watched my stepbrother get excited as he watched television. He then called me to the backroom and molested me. In Louisville, Kentucky, we have adult superstores and strip clubs—all these are legal. I cannot help but wonder how many women and children have been molested and raped as a direct result of a person going to one of these places.

Heres another one to think about: I am a recovering alcoholic and drug addict, and I attend twelve-step meetings on a regular basis. Our fellowship is in the millions. Almost all of us have families. There might be mothers, fathers, spouses, and children. Add that to the millions in our fellowship, and you will have but a small fraction of the people who have been harmed as a direct result of alcohol. I wonder if more people have died from a direct result of alcohol than all of the cancers put together. Moreover, ask yourself, why there are still breweries and distilleries? I cannot help but wonder why the mortality rate is not listed on the bottle. Does greed supersede life? Does it dictate acceptable numbers of deaths? The affects of sin in the physical sense is obviously catastrophic. Moreover, it is a contagious plague that spreads and grows way beyond a single act of a single person. The act of sin feeds evil, and I assure you, this evil grows. Unclean spirit is strong on this earth. It is fed an abundance of sin every day.

In looking back as a child at the sins that were directed toward me—the molestations and the beatings—there is absolutely no comparison in numbers to the hundreds, if not thousands, of people I have harmed through sin. This makes the sin toward me look small. This is what I mean when I say sin is a contagious plague which grows and spreads way beyond a single act of a single person.

Sin is sold on regular basis because it is bought. Sin is a high market item that seems to be the answer to all of our problems. Most all of my life I sought happiness through sin; I tried to be happy from the outside in. If you have read this book, then you know what has been produced. Sin seems to be the best marketing tool there is; if you want to sell something, put it on a television commercial beside a pretty woman who is half dressed. If that does not do it, then put a bottle of alcohol with her in the commercial. This will surely close a deal.

A person might read what I am writing and say I am going overboard with this and that if I don't like what is being sold on commercials, then don't buy what they're selling. My response would be, do they know what their selling? I am not trying to target the television or alcohol industry (this would be the cover up). If only these people could see firsthand the events that took place the day I was molested—to actually be able to see the lust as it grew in my stepbrother's eyes, to see the pain and confusion as it grew in my eyes. Now with all this said, I would be willing to bet if you asked my stepbrother why he molested me (unless he has had a spiritual awakening of some sort), his answer would be like mine as a child: "Because," or "I do not know." God bless him. We just do not know.

As a result of sin, I am not just spiritually blind, I am blind to all matters and I perceive the truth about nothing. I am like a newborn child whose eyes are still glazed over. My actions were dictated by impulse. My entire life has been a seek-and-destroy mission. It has been comparable to a long-range missile; I can push a button here and never see the destruction. Again, I will follow this with a simple question. Why? Is all this a result of which master I chose? Does the master of the house not control and take care of the house? Is this what drives impulse? (Anxiety and depression are constant companions of sin).

Now I will write about the spiritual effects of sin. The effects of sin in the spiritual sense is written a little differently. In a sense, it is blurry, and must be read with spiritual glasses. What I mean is this: we cannot perceive and understand spiritual matters through physical principals or laws. For example, in the physical, we categorize sin by the effects it has on people. We do this through a legal system; we take a spiritual matter, and belittle it by calling *sin,* a crime. We act as if these sins only affect the person, and the more pain that is inflicted on a person, the harsher the punishment. Where laws are an absolute necessity, we must look beyond the principals of law (to just begin to understand the spiritual effects of sin). In doing so, we get but a glimpse of the true spiritual effects of sin, and through this glimpse, a belief can be formed. Be careful. Just because we believe in something, that does not make it a spiritual truth. I had firm spiritual beliefs that were proven untrue through the spiritual laws of love. However, belief is good when we leave ourselves open to believe more. The spiritual glasses I referred to are made of faith, hope, and love. The frame is faith and hope, and the lenses from which we look and see are made of love. I have to believe that sin can effect something that I cannot see or perceive.

When I look at the effects of sin in the spiritual sense, I have to look beyond the effects it has on people and categorize sin by the effects it has on my relationship with God. In this respect, all sin seems to produce the same results; sin blocks us from God or truth. In Luke 23:34 after being nailed to the cross in Calvary, Jesus says: "Father forgive them, for they know not what they do." I cannot help but wonder if I could go back 2007 years and ask the question, "Why did you feel it necessary to nail Jesus to the cross?" if the answer would be similar to mine (because or I do not know). Jesus seems to think so. Spiritual law to me is absolutely incredible. It has lost none of its strength at all; the effects of sin are still binding. In the year of 2007, as a direct result of sin, men still know not what they do (still we nail each other to the cross). Do we know why? To think that the sin of murder is equal to the sin of lust, or even a sin that would seem smaller, like lying. This would probably anger a parent who has lost a child to a violent crime, especially if that parent—on his or her best of days—lies regularly. The parent could not possibly see it for what it is. On the cross, blood pouring from His hands and feet and in immense pain, Jesus still saw things as they were, spiritual. We all know that Jesus did not sin that day, not even a lie.

There are two employers in this world, God and Satan. God operates only in truth; Satan operates in deception. Satan would have us believe we are creatures of evolution. He would have us spend billions of dollars searching the stars for proof, knowing that we cannot prove God to each other. That proof is internal, not external. God cannot be found in the heavens, rather in the hearts.

An owner of a grocery store would have several employees. He would have shelf stockers, cashiers, and people to sweep and mop the floors. He would also have a manager and maybe an assistant manager. Some may seem more important than others, like the manager for example, because he is familiar with all operation of the whole store. The person cleaning the floors knows only this. However, when asked, the owner would surely agree that all his employees are necessary. Satan operates the same way. He needs all of his employees. The seven deadly sins are nothing for his managers, and when necessary, the assistant manager can take over. His cashiers and shelf stockers have special talents, maybe lust and anger. Whereas the floor cleaner only lies, and still he reaps a liar's pay; he is blocked from God and truth.

I would now like to take a moment and explain why I have written so much about Satan or unclean spirit if you prefer. Throughout my life I have heard how hard it is to live a spiritual life. It seems to demand perfection. If that were true, I surely would not be writing this book. Perfection is a stumbling block laid by Satan himself. My goal has been to love God and all people. that is God's will for all of us, as it was spoken by Jesus. What happens and what I become as a result of this goal is a direct result of the spiritual law of love, and it remains true for every person.

I have found that through my own experience living a spiritual life is in fact easy, and the benefits are incredible. The struggle, the confusion, the very battle itself is in trying to leave the unspiritual life; it would be comparable to trying to leave the mafia. Satan would rather have us dead than serve God. In the beginning of this journey, I told God I would do anything he wanted me to do, just show me how. Not only has God shown me how to live a spiritual life, He has shown me how to leave the unspiritual life. In building a spiritual life, it is important that we try and remove the things that bind us to this physical world. It is also important that we know to whom these things belong.

I hope that what I have written so far can help a person identify the things that are used to build walls around God. My hope is that I have sparked interest in the reader that we might think outside of what seems normal, that maybe things are far more spiritual than what they appear to be, and that maybe there is more inside of me than just me.

Again, I have hope that everything that I write from this point on will give you, the reader, hope in love. This hope can be used as a vessel, which would lead us to God's purpose for our very existence (to learn and then live a life of abundant and everlasting love). Inside of every man and woman is a desire that supersedes all other desires; it is the desire for love. Search yourself and see if it is not there. When you find it, ask yourself how it got there. Then, thank God. Remember God is love.

Finally, I will write about love. I believe in writing this book, I have given the reader a somewhat accurate depiction of the man that I was. If I was not a manager for Satan, then surely I was a good assistant manager. While I have never killed a person, my desires were to do just that. There were times when my intent was to kill a person. I also believe if I were given the right set of circumstances, anything was possible through me. I was a mean and evil man.

I would now like to try to give an accurate depiction of the man that I am now, as a result of God and love. If you could take a moment and think of the bad things I have done, take another and think about how I can say I love the men who molested me. I love the men who killed my brother. As a matter of fact, I love everybody. How does a man do this? How does he change like this? It is my belief that the man himself does not change. The change that occurs is in the spirit, which resides in a man (man being but a house). Sure, the desire and willingness has to be there to prompt this change. However, what is it that changes?

I would like to back this up with a small story. As I have stated in this book, there were times when I really wanted to change specific things about myself. If I would add these up, there would be a long list of desired changes. However, what about the things I did not want to change? Most of my life I never liked or respected animals. As a matter of fact, sometimes I would kill them just to watch them die. Sometimes I would shoot birds just to see there feathers go "poof," and I hated cats. I live on a small farm, and I have animals. I have a chicken, a dog, a puppy, five cats, and three kittens. Almost one year ago, one of my cats came up missing. On the second day I found myself walking my property yelling, "Here kitty, kitty. Here kitty, kitty." Then it dawned on me what I was doing and how worried I was over a cat. I stopped in my tracks, and I asked God what He had done to me. Within one second, I had the answer. Within one more second, I was on my knees in tears thanking Him for what He had done. I also have a puppy. Her name is Boo Boo. To just see this pup brings a smile to my face. I love her so much that at times it brings tears to my eyes. Can you imagine how much more I love people? This is a result of a change of spirit, not a change of man. It is way too big for men.

I had no desire to love these animals, it just happened; however, this is one small piece of a much larger puzzle. As I proceed in this chapter, I will write in detail about what has happened to me as a result of love. I will write about both the physical and spiritual senses, as both of these areas have been drastically transformed. Last week I watched an animated movie called Ice Age: Meltdown. In the beginning of this movie, there where three major players: a sloth, a tiger, and a mammoth. The mammoth thought it was the only one left on the planet and was in search of another mammoth. In finding a female mammoth, the male mammoth was stumped. The female mammoth thought she was an opossum, and she had two opossum brothers. He set out to prove to her that she was a mammoth. After several failed attempts, she finally got it. And this is what she said, "What a crazy day. I woke up an opossum, and now I am a mammoth."

I got a good laugh from this animated movie. However, this is what it was like for me. I woke up one day—a shell of a man, in immense pain, and broken in a way that I believed was beyond repair—and through the power of love, I was transformed back into my original state, the very state that God intended for us all. I have been transformed into a child of God. This transformation did not happen overnight, and it is still not over. However, more things happened the day I asked God for help than I could possibly see at the time. My desire to drink and take drugs left me that day. More importantly, my desire to hurt people left me that very day. For these desires to stay gone, I have to continually work to maintain myself spiritually.

At the time, all this seemed to come at a price (the destruction of self). It seemed a high price to pay. However, was I comparing apples to apples? Why did it seem to be a struggle to give up a life that had not only failed, but also left a path of destruction in its wake? The spiritual life is not something to be bought or traded for. The spiritual life is something to fight for, and the fight is internal, not external. In the animated movie, the mammoth only thought she was a oppossum. She had always been a mammoth. What a wonderful day when she realized what she really was. It was through love that I realized what I really was and always had been; it is only now that I see spiritually.

I remember a few years ago talking to my friend and spiritual advisor about love. We talked about love being like a radio wave which could, in fact, link any person to God. Love has since proven itself to do exactly that and so much more. I do not want to get ahead of myself, so I will go back to the beginning. The day I cried to God, asking Him to please help, on that very day at that very moment, God imposed a thought in me that was not mine: "Calvin, I have always loved you." I know this was God because my life has not been the same since. When the love of God finally reaches its destination and strokes a person on there heart, that person will never be the same again.

The pain and suffering, the guilt, depression, and shame of my past were all lifted for that moment, and for the first time in over thirty years, I could see the good things in life. For a moment, my vision had cleared, and I could see things as they are, *spiritual*. All the bad things that this world had to offer had vanished for that moment. It was as if I were an infant, experiencing life with a joy and enthusiasm that only a child can have. With the same magic that made these things appear, they would now disappear, leaving only one thing behind, a desire.On page 116, I wrote about a desire that supersedes all other desires; that desire is for love. From that day on, I knew the definition of love was God. From that day on, I have sought God with the overwhelming desire for His love.

In chapter seven, I wrote about God prompting me to speak. I also wrote about feeling the presence of God as I was walking in the rain to a mission to eat. The amazing thing to me is that I was not that far into this journey, and my awareness of God was becoming more defined. I was now feeling His presence in the physical sense. Looking back at this, I know that my desire to love God and all people has not yet been established. I believe what has prompted this awareness is God's love for me coupled with my desire to seek and love God and not hurt people. To make our beginning in love, we must first try to stop hurting people. For me, this was a lot harder than it sounds. I have not mastered it by any means. What I have mastered is my apology. Sometimes my awareness of God is as simple as setting right my wrongs. This is where I feel so blessed to have a twelve-step program to help me identify some of the things about myself that are blocking me from God (sin).

For a while, I could only feel the presence of God in the physical sense. It is my belief that most people stop here, maybe believing they have reached the highest level of awareness of God that is possible on this earth. That level being to physically feel the presence of God (a tangible feeling of God's presence). I believe for a while I had fallen prey to this self-imposed spiritual trap. There were times when I felt the presence of God profoundly; it felt as if I had a force field around me. At other times I felt light, almost as if I could float. As I became more and more aware of this feeling, I became curious as to why it was happening. I decided to pay attention to what was going on around me when I felt this presence of God. What I noticed is at this heightened state of awareness, my thoughts and concerns were for other people. Right in the middle of trying to help someone, I would feel the presence of God. When I had an overwhelming desire to help my fellow man (with no selfish interest), this would prompt the feeling of the presence of God.

For a while, all was well, and then I began to slowly lose these feelings. I believe I became complacent in my own mind. I thought I had arrived at God's doorstep. Whatever I was doing at the time seemed good enough. My spiritual growth came to a slow crawl. Two things snapped me to my senses: one, my desire to feel God's love, and two, my desire to love God. Shortly after this, God commissioned me to write this book about love, but only after I could love all people. I believe God knew that if I could manage to love all people, I would surely write this book. To achieve this level of love, and then try to contain it in the house that I call a body is impossible. I am in fact writing this book, and I assure you it is not enough. Love is so expansive that I have to talk about it every day. Every day I pray, I meditate, and I think about love. My thoughts are consumed with God, love, and my fellow man. I assure you this is not me; this is love in its true form (spiritual). On a good day, I wanted to murder people; on a God day, I wanted to love people. These two statements seem drastically different, as if they should not come from the same person, and that is my point. As a result of love, I am not the same person.

After God commissioned me to love all people, I thought, What a challenge. Can this actually be done? At the time, I was capable of being a little objective about myself. I thought that I loved some people; however, I knew I did not love all people. In fact, some people I did not even like. What I found out is this: love dose not operate in halves; I could not love half the people and hate the other half. It is okay to progressively love more and more people when your desire is to love all people. This would be spiritual growth. It was after studying a book called *Expanding Love* by the Dali Lama and practicing the meditations in this book that I would soon find out how selective I was of people and how little I knew about love and its effects. This book challenged me to wish well on people who had harmed me, and I could not do it. At the time, I was sure I had forgiven these people, but now I knew I had not. Then the thought hit me, how can I love the men who killed my brother? How can I love the men who molested me? How do we love people we hate?

At the time, I did not know how to answer these questions. What I did know is that God had put it on my heart to love all of these people. I knew for sure that day that this would happen, that I would in fact love all of these people. The miracle of this moment is this: although I did not love these people yet, the mere thought of it brought a peace upon me that was beyond my understanding.

God had given me direction. I now had something to focus on. I knew in my heart that to love the men who had killed my brother would, in fact, be the long awaited answer to a thousand questions. As I set out to do this, there seemed to be something new about me. I believe this new thing was happiness in its true form (spiritual). I would like to say that all went well and that there were no problems as I set out to love these men; however, there were a lot of problems and little progress. There seemed to be a struggle within. At times, I thought I must be going in the wrong direction. I thought that God's will for me would not be so complicated, and it would be easier. I had fallen prey to this kind of thinking several times, but this time, I was spiritually prepared for battle. I have heard so many people (including myself) say, "God's will for me would not cause so much pain and confusion," and I would totally abandon the direction I was going.

This time, I would stay the course. Usually pain and confusion were by-products of my negative actions (sin and seperation from God). This was different. My thoughts and actions were consumed with love. The pain and confusion was coming from somewhere else. In New Testament scripture (Ephesians 6:10-13), it states, "Finally, my brethren, be strong in the Lord and in the powers of His might. Put on the whole armor of God, that you may be able to stand against the wiles of the devil. For we do not wrestle against the flesh and blood, but against principalities, against powers, against the rulers of the darkness of this age, against spiritual hosts of wickedness in the heavenly places. Therefore take up the whole armor of God, that you may be able to withstand in the evil day, and having done all to stand."

This is what I was up against: powers, rulers of darkness, and spiritual hosts of wickedness. This sure seems like a lot to chew on, but I assure you it is true. Satan knew if I could love the men I hated the most, he would in fact be found out. My awareness of God and Satan depended on whether or not I could love these people.

The answer to loving all people came to me through prayer and meditation. This day of prayer and meditation was prompted by my desire for God's love. On that particular day, I wanted to be closer to God. I knew that I could be, I just did not know how, so I prayed about it. Again, the answer came to me through a thought, which I knew was not mine: "Calvin, if you want to get closer to Me, get closer to people, for there, I am." It took a few days for this to sink in; however, when it did, it hit me deep. I knew that day that there was a piece of God in all of us, not just the people I considered good people, but all people. The labels that I would put on people through judgement (whether they are good people or bad) had no bearing on God whatsoever. Again, God is the creator. To put his mark on his creation seemed fitting to me. The fact that He put a piece of Himself in all people it truly our blessing. In Luke 17:20-21 it states: "Now when He was asked by the Pharisees when the kingdom of God would come, He answered them and said, 'The kingdom of God does not come with observation nor will they say, see here! Or see there! For indeed, the kingdom of God is within you.'"

This thought that God has given me would be the missing key that would unlock my ability to love the very people I hated. After this thought settled in, I believed and knew that God was in all people. When I looked for Him there, slowly but surely I could see

Him. This is what I meant in chapter nine when I said I could see a thousand miracles a day, I only need to open my eyes. I could see God in people. To think that fellowship with God is as simple as fellowshipping with His people. As this thought became a reality for me, it became easy to love the men who had killed my brother and the men who had molested me. It became easy to love my aggressors. While I am not yet in a constant state of love, most times I can love my aggressors before they arrive, and if not, then shortly after.

The day that I realized that I loved these men, a lot of things began to change. Things that I considered absolute truths became untrue as truth was revealed. Freedom would be an understatement when trying to explain the release from the spiritual bondage that I was in, especially when you do not know you're bound. Happiness, joy, and peace—these words all had new definitions. They became a working part of myself as I employed their maker, love. To me, this could be comparable to an angel who's wings have just sprouted, and the angel cannot wait to fly. I could not wait to spread this love. My hope is that the very men who I have struggled to love can in fact love me as much as I love them—that they indeed can love God and all people; that they may experience the fruit of the tree of life (love); and that they may know the happiness, joy, and peace as they are plucked from His branches.

This in fact would be a turning point in my life. As I fill myself with love, I perceive and understand spiritual matters. As my desire and ability to love grows, it is matched with spiritual understanding and a profound and growing awareness of God within me. Gradually I am becoming aware of what I really am, and equally as important, what I am not. I have lived most of my life trying to understand and perceive all matters through physical principals. For example, one apple plus two apples equals three apples. As people, we try to understand spiritual matters through physical principals. It is so easy to judge our spiritual growth by our physical surroundings. If

I have a nice car, a nice house, and money in the bank, it is easy to say, "God has surely blessed me. I must be doing something right." As always, I have judged myself by the world's standards, i.e., all things are judged by the affects they have on me. When using this measuring stick, spiritual blindness is absolute. I will go further in saying that faith and hope are spiritual in nature, but only as they are used to activate love. Love is the greatest of the three, as stated in 1 Corinthians. I have heard so many people say we are called to faith, but this is a spiritual trap. We are called to the highest of all callings, which is love. To stay contained in faith and hope for years without a continual growth in love is to stay contained in this physical world—to never know the spiritual truth. It is to settle for someone else's beliefs, as we are taught them by our fellow man (as he was taught it). Are we still in the dark? In the spiritual world, one apple plus two apples can equal one thousand apples (*remember this, in the gospel of Matthew 15-34 seven loaves and a few fish, fed four thousand*). Love alone teaches us this spiritual math. Love is the interpreter of all spiritual truth.

In chapter ten, I stated that knowledge, wisdom, and truth were poured out upon us, as a result of love. I also stated that we could now see physical and spiritual. In chapter nine, I wrote about God wanting to keep me out of scripture for a while. I believe God's intentions were to show me that He had in fact written the book of life, the book of all knowledge, wisdom, and truth. In finishing this, He then installed and locked it in the hearts of every man and woman. He then gave us the ability to create the key through our actions and associations with God and His people. He did this so that it could open our hearts. That key is made of love. As I progressed in love, things within me continually changed. Yet still I was spiritually bound. I could but glimpse at the truth through eyes that could not yet perceive and understand spiritual matters. However, because of this quest for love, I was given enough understanding to know there was a whole lot more to this spiritual stuff than I could have possibly imagined.

On the day that I realized that I loved all people, not just the men who had offended me, but all people—even people I have yet to meet—I loved God that day as a whole, not in parts, as He is spread about in people. I loved God in his entirety, as He is in all people. On that day, the forty years of accumulated knowledge that I had acquired (good and bad) were erased. On that day, my heart was open, and the book of life was revealed. On that day, I changed. I know now how Saul, the man in scripture who stoned Christians to their deaths, was changed into Paul. This is the very man who wrote almost half of the twenty-seven books in the New Testament, and had he lived longer, I believe he would have written more. It is this kind of change that I am talking about.

I have since become aware of God in such a way that in the allness of His presence, I weep with overwhelming joy. I have yet to see God, but I know His spirit as it moves in and through me. Although this body is bound to this earth and is physical in appearance, what is inside of it is not. Throughout scripture, there is talk of a Holy Spirit, the spirit of truth, and the kingdom of God being within us. Would God give us such wonderful gifts as these with no means of recognizing them? Although I live on this earth, I am no longer bound by it. The spirit that I feed is of God, not Satan.

I hope that I have not discouraged anyone from reading and studying scripture. That has not been my intent, just the opposite. My hope is that as we study and teach scripture, its message will carry through to the hearts of people. My hope is that as these people apply its principal of love, they too will be set free spiritually. That they may be unbound by their actions and any teachings that would impose limits on their spiritual abilities or limit the nature of God's miracles. After all, the miracles are His to give.

As you can tell, I read and study scripture today, and it is an absolute joy to do so. However, I am still amazed by the fact that I knew the truth of scripture before I read it. As you read this book, you might be thinking, "Man, this person is out of his mind." On the other hand, you might believe what I have written and leave it alone. Either way, do yourself the favor of finding out for yourself. Please do not trust me. Prove God to yourself. Set out to love God and all people and see for yourself what happens, and as you do so, simply believe that what has happened to me can happen to you.

In chapter nine I stated if a person could love God and all people, that person would have no need to go to heaven, that heaven would come to that person. What I meant in that statement is this: I am aware of God in me. There are days when I look out on this earth, at all that beauty that He has created, and as I look, He shares my eyes with me, and I am aware of Him. In harmony, we share this body. In my heart, I know I have found what my soul has been in search of. I have found my creator, my father. In His house are many mansions. Search yourself over with eyes that love, and you too shall find Him, waiting with arms open, ready to receive you. Of all the places to look, the kingdom of God is within.

I believe the final stage of a miracle from God is for man to receive and then acknowledge the miracle—to look beyond what men might think and speak the truth from the heart. That is what I have done in this book; I have spoken the truth from my heart, as God has put it there. I expect people will oppose what I have written. Others will challenge it. Please do, the only true way to prove me wrong is to try to prove me right. Love God and all people, and see what happens!

Love in its true form (spiritual) bridges a gap, which can take a human being from a physical belief into a spiritual reality. Although there are many roads to love, (faith and hope) once there, love is the only vessel that can travel the distance to a man's heart. It is there that we find God, and it is then that we become aware of our at oneness with God. As I have become aware of God in the literal sense, I have been struck dumb. There is no physical explanation as to what has happened to me. It is beyond understanding, yet worth believing. As spiritual truth is revealed, a humbleness that is coupled with joy, peace, and an overall sense of wellbeing is constant.

In scripture, John 14:20-23, Jesus states, "At that day you will know that I am in the father and you in me, and I in you. He who has my commandments and keeps them, it is he who loves me. And he who loves me will be loved by my father, and I will love him and manifest myself in him. Judas not Iscariot said to him, 'Lord how is that you will manifest yourself to us, and not the world?' Jesus answered and said to him, 'If anyone loves me, he will keep my word; and my father will love him, and we will come to him and make our home with him.'"

Jesus has given us only two commandments. In short, they are to love God and (all) people. In addition, to those who could achieve these commands, He has given a promise, and He states it twice: one, "And I will love him and manifest myself in him; and two, "And my father will love him, and we will come to him and make our home with him." The thing that I would like to impose on the reader is that we become aware of this manifestation of God and Jesus. As we are aware of our thoughts and as we are aware of the sun as it rises, we become aware of God's indwelling presence as He moves within us. It is unmistakable. I could not miss it, and to go forward, I simply had to acknowledge this miracle from God.

Where I have stated that God's presence was unmistakable and that I could not miss it, I also could not understand it. It would be comparable to looking at an empty glass at one moment, and in the next moment—without ever taking my eyes off it—the glass is full. There is no one-plus-two-equals-three explanation as to how this happens. There is no physical explanation to this matter simply because this process is spiritual in nature. Spiritual law supersedes physical law.

In closing this chapter and finishing this book, I have a few closing statements. The first is this: in chapter 7, I stated that I did not have to come to God at the church pew and confess Jesus, and that is a true statement. I believe God wanted me to go around that and come to Jesus through love. As a result of the practice of love, I came into a collision course with Jesus. I now would highly recommend that a person confess Jesus as quickly as possible, whether it be at a church pew or in your backyard, it does not matter.

The second statement is this; for the majority of my life I could see no reason to love the people who had harmed me: it made no sense at all for me to do this. I could see no benefit in this at all. The reason it made no sense is because I was looking for personal gain, rather then spiritual gain. What could a person possibly gain from loving someone who has harmed him so deeply? In my mind, this act of love would cause more grief and more pain. In reality, the lack of this love would cause the pain and grief. Moreover, it would not stay contained in the boundaries of myself. This pain would explode outward by way of anger toward countless others, causing more pain and suffering than the original offense.

In the first thought of loving all people, there seemed to be a huge amount of self-sacrifice involved. So much in fact, that it seemed that I would surely lose. Let's take a look at what I have actually lost: anxiety, anger, rage, resentment, fear, and depression. Where have they gone? What about my desire to steal and harm others? What happened to me? Animals are even safe around me now. Where have I gone? My point is this: when we look at the results, love is not hard on a person. It is easy. By losing these things, I have not been left void or empty; I have in fact been filled. I am in the company of a profound master of peace. His love provides all my needs. I am in the company of our father, and this will lead to my final statement.

All my life I have believed that there was a God, although there were times when I was hoping there was not, yet still I believed. However, belief is just belief; there is no hard fact in it. Where all the evidence seemed to me to imply there was a God, I was sure a man would have to die a physical death to know the truth or not. I have joyfully been proven wrong. A person need only achieve love as Jesus commanded, and He and the father will come to that person wherever he or she is. It is in the death of the body that we go to Jesus and the father where they are.

I tell you, there is a profound peace in knowing the truth. It is beyond explaining. God never intended for us stay in the dark. He sent Jesus to teach us how to turn on the light. The lesson He taught was unconditional love. If a man can achieve this love and God and Jesus would make their home with him here on this earth, then surely that man's ticket to eternal life with God is bought and paid for.

The greatest gifts from God are wrapped in love. I wonder how many of these gifts are left unclaimed. I wonder how many people will refuse to love God and all people. I will close this book in saying that I claimed my gift. To receive love, we have to give it. Remember, God is love. It is on this chariot that we ride to heaven.

Thank you, God

Thank you, Jesus.

The Plea

It has been several months that have passed since I finished writing this book. In that time, I have felt a void within myself that proclaims to me: "You are not done. There is more." There is an experience that I have had recently that I would profess to be an act of God. This experience would acknowledge what the void in me had already proclaimed—I was not done writing.

I do not know what to call this experience, whether it was a vision from God or some sort of premonition. What I do know is it was spiritually based and from God. The experience was this: I was driving in my truck, a normal and familiar route. At one moment, all was normal. In the next, it was as if I had driven into a new dimension. It was comparable to driving into a ghost town. The scenery was the same and all of life was there, yet it was full of death. It was as if the eyes of people had been sewn shut. We were oblivious to our actions as we destroyed one another in spirit and in flesh.

In truth, I did not drive into a new dimension that day, I drove into reality. God let me see the fullness of sin that day. It was like driving into a thick fog that was invisible to the naked eye. It was only seen through the eye of the heart. In this, it was magnified by a thousand times over. I could essentially see what had been invisible. As I drove through this sin, I felt the pain of this earth and still do today. As I drew near to my destination, I drove out of this fog of sin and again lost vision of it.

In my heart, I believe that by and through the power of love and the grace of God, I was able to see the fullness of sin—more importantly, to drive through it. Had I not had my fill of love that day, surely I would have fell. Moreover, I would have been blind to what caused me to fall.

Since that day, my thoughts have written a few more pages to this book. I have called these pages, "The Plea." There is good reason for this title. I believe God has conditioned my heart to make His plea to all people. What is His plea? Is it about our kids who are shot and killed by their classmates? Or our wives who are killed by drunk drivers, as they drive home from work? What about the man who commits suicide after finding his wife with another man? Is this worthy of a plea? How about the tens of thousands that die annually to some sort of addiction, whether it be cigarettes or crack cocaine. Maybe I should not mention the homeless people who die under bridges or in plastic houses in the woods. What about the men and women worldwide who stand across from one another, firing their weapons with the sole intention of killing each other? Then, they profess this action to be in the interest of peace or God.

What is God's plea? It is a simple request, yet very painful. God is pleading that we stop killing each other. I have a friend and spiritual advisor who I have mentioned in this book. I have talked to him several times about the feeling of the presence of God as it covers me. This feeling is so profound that my teeth chatter and tears pour out of my eyes as God cries through me. It feels as if God is trying to speak through me. These feelings are manifested and made to activate by one thought. That's right, one thought makes this happen, peace. The thought of peace; a day when men refuse to kill each other.

If God is love as stated in first John, then God surely feels. Love feels the pain and joy of others. God feels the loss of each of His children and rejoices in the hope of their peace. From the beginning of this book, I have been brought to tears by the thought of the impact of love and of its final reward (peace). The greatest men of this earth knew that peace could only be achieved through love.

I am thinking back to my childhood and about my school. There was no metal detector to scan for weapons. Kids were not being shot in schools in the early seventies. In the mid-eighties, flying 747s into buildings and killing thousands of innocent people did not seem to be a part of any strategical military plan that I had heard of. People being shot to death in our city streets was not an everyday event as it is now. What I am trying to say here is this: if I look back over the last thirty-five years of my life, I can see clearly the progression of sin through the accumulation of death. Like Siamese twins who are joined at the hip, death and sin walk hand and hand.

I consider myself to be a fairly spiritual man. While at home, I pray, meditate, and study scripture. I try to fill myself with as much love as I possibly can before I leave home. It is a reserve that is well needed. My goal is to make it back home feeling the same way I did when I left. Most times, I succeed, but sometimes, I fail utterly. There are days when I have to stop and pray for strength—several times in one day. I am tempted that much.

It seems that life is built around the thrust of sin, designed to tell me what I need—more sex, more money, a nicer car, one drink, or a new medication. The list goes on forever. For every man or woman who strives to climb the spiritual ladder to freedom, there are hundreds of others who will pull them down. Why? Can we not see what we are doing to one another? Does the master distiller not see that tens of thousands are dying annually due to his drink? Are our eyes sewn shut? Do we care?

I am convinced (as God has revealed to me the true nature of people) that we are by nature essentially good. It should not be a struggle to let this good shine. In the last five years, I have learned to love people who have harmed me deeply. I have come to love people I have yet to meet. As a result of this kind of love, I have been covered in a blanket of peace. This peace surpassed my understanding; I have never known anything like this. How could I? I had never known love.

God's plea is not much to ask. Before we can know peace, we have to stop hurting each other. This can allow love to settle in. In the book of Isaiah, chapter 65, he talks about the creation of a new heaven and a new earth. In chapter 65 verse 25, it states: "The wolf and the lamb will feed together. The lion will eat hay like the cow. But the snakes will eat dust." Is this to say we will eat at peace with our enemies? You have to admit that sure sounds good.

As I have stated, I love the men who molested me and the men who killed my brother. I love all the people who died in the world trade centers, including the men who flew the planes. What about the men and women in the battlefields and their families, do I love them? Of course, I do, on both sides,too. Who will follow this lead? Who will say I love the man who raped me or I love the insurgent who shot my son or I love the man who took my job or I love the lady who ran me off the road?

For sin to be activated and then cause death, people have to participate. For love to be activated, and then cause peace, people have to participate! In the beginning of my journey with God, I cried a simple prayer. As I pleaded to God, it went like this:

Oh

God

Please

Help

Since that day, I participated in what I believed God would have me do, and since then, every day of my life has gotten better.

In His plea, God has asked me to deliver a prayer to you from Him. It is a simple prayer, it goes like this:

Oh

People

Please

Help

Who will participate in love, to produce peace?

May God's love fill you full.

Printed in the United States
145931LV00001B/102/P